Authentic Cosmopolitanism

Authentic Cosmopolitanism

Love, Sin, and Grace in the Christian University

R. J. SNELL

and

STEVEN D. CONE

PICKWICK *Publications* · Eugene, Oregon

AUTHENTIC COSMOPOLITANISM
Love, Sin, and Grace in the Christian University

Pickwick Publications
An Imprint of Wipf and Stock Publishers
199 W. 8th Ave., Suite 3
Eugene, OR 97401

www.wipfandstock.com

ISBN 13: 978-1-61097-365-6

Cataloging-in-Publication data:

Snell, R. J., 1975–

 Authentic cosmopolitanism : love, sin, and grace in the Christian university / R. J. Snell and Steven D. Cone.

 xii + 190 p. ; 23 cm. Including bibliographical references.

 ISBN 13: 978-1-61097-365-6

 1. Christian education. 2. Education—Religious aspects. I. Cone, Steven D. II. Title.

LC538 .S62 2013

Manufactured in the U.S.A.

For Fred and Sue Lawrence,
teachers of collaboration

Contents

Humans = lovers

Integral unity

Preface

Authentic - blch

ONE CERTAINLY CANNOT COMPLAIN that the evangelical community, broadly construed, is unreflective about higher education; indeed, there is something of a cottage industry outlining the rise, collapse, and nature of Christian higher education. Many other texts explore the vocation of the Christian scholar and teacher and the value and limits of teaching a Christian worldview. And recent years have seen the emergence of books tracing alternative models of Christian higher education rooted in a variety of denominational traditions and practices.

While these previous volumes have served admirably in the maturation of evangelicals concerning Christian higher education, for which we owe their authors an enormous debt, the conversation on Christian higher education (1) tends to retain an inadequate theological anthropology and metaphysics of the person, (2) tends to overlook or ignore a phenomenological account of concrete human persons in favor of abstractions about worldview, (3) suffers from an inadequate epistemology which forgets the real effects of sin and grace on the intellect, and (4) struggles to fully incorporate intellectual pursuits and moral formation into an overarching *telos* for the university. This book intends to ameliorate those problems.

These shortcomings can be resolved by returning again to Augustine, or at least Augustine in conversation with Aquinas, Martin Heidegger, the overlooked Jesuit thinker Bernard Lonergan, and the important contemporary Charles Taylor. For these thinkers, an examination of the concrete human subject reveals that persons are, first and foremost, lovers. The Western tradition is full of attempts to consider humans as intellects first, forgetting that knowledge is made possible and intelligible by desire, by the moral and intentional horizons of the phenomenological subject. An account of the human as lover not only solves the issues identified above but also provides a normative vision for Christian higher education by revealing an authentic order to love—loves, made authentic by grace, allow the intellectually, morally, and religiously converted person to attain an integral unity. Properly understanding the integral relation between love and the fullness of human life overcomes the split between intel-

ix

lectual and moral formation, allowing transformed subjects—authentic lovers—to live, seek, and work towards the values of a certain kind of cosmopolitanism. Christian universities exist to make cosmopolitans, properly understood, namely, those persons capable of living authentically. In other words, this text gives a full-orbed account of *human flourishing*, rooted in a phenomenological account of the human, as basis for the mission of the university.

An introduction summarizes contemporary discourse on Christian higher education and outlines its oversights before turning in Part One to notions of intellectual conversion and the authentic order of love. Augustine very famously struggles in the *Confessions* to overcome his difficulties with God and evil. Assuming that God, as all reality, must be material, he simply cannot believe in God, and he undergoes a shocking intellectual conversion whereby he understands why reality need not be material. In *De Trinitate*, especially the sections on the psychological analogy, Augustine explains how the inner word is formed from memory by the workings of love, something Aquinas develops. Augustine and Aquinas provide an integral vision of human knowledge and action whereby properly ordered love precedes intellect and results in ordered action, knowledge, and life. This theological anthropology, fleshed out in conversation with Plato, Heidegger, Taylor, and Lonergan, provides an understanding of the subject grounded in the concrete and dynamic nature of human knowing and loving, and therefore also offers a phenomenologically grounded notion of the human self toward which education ought to be oriented.

Part Two continues with an exploration of the need for what Augustinians of a certain bent call moral and religious conversion whereby God's love so alters our phenomenological and moral horizons as to remake our subjectivity. Of course to understand this we'll need first to provide an account of the noetic effects of sin, i.e., how sin impairs reason through the disordering of love. Augustine's account of concupiscence and pride, seen in *Confessions* and *On Free Will* and taken up by Aquinas in the *Summa*, grounds an explanation of how different aspects of disordered desire distort us. If the first part gives something analogous to nature/creation, Part Two gives something like fall and redemption, but in a particular mode, namely that of the phenomenology of sin and grace for the human subject. For it is the grace of God's love that ultimately establishes the rectitude of our desiring, and as rightly ordered lovers we are motivated and enabled to pursue authentic relations to value and truth.

Part Three explains how a remaking of the order of love in intellectual, moral, and religious conversion provides a normative, but non-abstract, vision of human development and authenticity, especially in the domain of value ethics, and provides the heuristic of educating for cosmopolis. The text concludes with suggested principles for the conversation on higher education. The Christian university is uniquely positioned to fulfill the vocation of "university"—the flourishing of the human spirit—if it understands and integrates the right ordering of love with moral and intellectual excellence.

This book is intended for a serious and educated readership, but not for specialists. All those interested in Christian higher education, the liberal arts, formation, philosophy, contemporary political theory, ethics, and theology would find something of interest without needing to have previously read the thinkers discussed. Certainly this is not a book only for those in the university, for concerned as we are with education this is not a text with concrete proposals for university life. No curricula or programs or initiatives are suggested, and we provide no classroom suggestions or even a philosophy of education. Instead we provide an answer to who and what we are as humans and a critically grounded account of what it means for human persons to flourish as persons and the consequences of sin and grace in our flourishing. As such, the text can be read as dealing with a foundational project rather than application, although we're quite confident of the consequences for application. But one could read the text with or without an eye to education; in any event, we are looking to the first principles, for the anthropology, without fail, will shape the pedagogy.

* * *

No text is written alone, and we acknowledge the support and assistance of many, including our colleagues at Eastern University, Lincoln Christian University, the Templeton Honors College, and the Agora Institute, especially those helpful interlocutors spurring thought forward: Drew Alexander, Phil Cary, Austin Detwiler, Jeff Dill, James Estep, Joe Gordon, Kelly Hanlon, Clay Ham, Ryan Hemmer, Sarah Moon, Amy Richards, Justin Schwartz, Christopher Simpson, Seth Thomas, Neal Windham,

Jonathan Yonan, and the members of the LCU Writer's Club. Many thanks for the assistance of the staff at Pickwick publications, especially our editor, Charlie Collier. Finally, we owe much gratitude to supportive families: Amy, Grace, Mather, Clara, and Emma Snell, and Violeta and Anna Cone.

Thinkers or Lovers

A Brief Introduction

Those of us involved with higher education, and perhaps especially those in Christian higher education, sometimes appear fixated on the subject of what we do exactly, and why. Every year finds more books and articles on the goals and purposes of the university, and a good many begin with an apologetic asking "why another book on the Christian university?"[1] It might not seem an exaggeration to claim that the purpose of a university appears to be conversation about the purpose of a university—exactly the sort of self-reflexive circle causing joy for philosophers and exasperation for vice presidents of finance.

Within the orbit of Christian higher education, especially but not only within evangelical circles, a conception of higher education known as *the integration model* has served as something like the default position, or at least "has largely defined the terms and delineated the boundaries of the current conversation."[2] In fact, because the past work of thinkers such as George Marsden, Nicholas Wolterstorff, and Arthur Homes was so "visible and so compelling, it is easy to imagine that the . . . [integration] model for Christian higher education is the only available model."[3] It would be somewhat of a simplification, but accurate in the main, to say that many starting points for reflection about education have depended heavily on an earlier generation of thinkers, often Reformed in theology and thought, who provided a thoughtful model for integrating faith and learning.

Despite its prevalence, the integration model does not translate well into every denominational or theological context, and the various

1. See, as examples, Benne, *Quality with Soul*; Budde and Wright, *Conflicting Allegiances*; Burtchaell, *Dying of the Light*; Cunningham, *To Teach*; Holmes, *The Idea of a Christian College*; MacIntyre, *God, Philosophy, Universities*.

2. Jacobsen and Hustedt Jacobsen, *Scholarship and Christian Faith*, 16.

3. Hughes, *Models for Christian Higher Education*, 5.

thinkers vs lovers

church and school traditions, even while gratefully acknowledging their dependence and benefit, are now moving beyond it, or at least attempting to augment the discussion in new and diverse directions.[4] For some, *Is this an accurate description?* the expansion is a matter of theological heritage, with the integration model viewed as Reformed, committed to the sovereignty of God over all dimensions of human act and knowledge, whereas a Mennonite commitment to radical discipleship, a Lutheran hesitation to blur distinctions between the kingdoms, or a Roman Catholic commitment to the integrity and autonomy of the world does not necessarily fit the model.[5]

It is not our intention here to re-trace the history of integration or its expansion, as other works adequately do so. We are, however, interested in exploring one particularly compelling question emerging in the pushback against integration, namely, whether we define ourselves primarily as *thinkers* or as *lovers*.

An extensive tradition views humans as primarily or especially thinking beings or rational animals, and education so influenced is largely concerned with the making of minds, dissemination of ideas, analysis of worldviews, research and dissemination of information, critical thinking, or even the integration of faith and reason. If education exists primarily for the in-forming of minds, the highest good sought will be a contemplative one.[6] The chancellor of Boston College, J. Donald Monan, explains the implications:

> This presuppoꜱite, quite simply, is that liberal education is directed almost exclusively at the intellects of students; that it is the communication of truths and skills and habits and qualities of intellect—as though keenness and method in knowing and voluminousness in one's learning constitutes one liberally educated . . . But to set the purpose of education outside of knowl-

---

4. These next several paragraphs draw heavily from the work of Peterson and Snell, "Faith Forms the Intellectual Task," 215–17. They include the following sources as representing the broadening of discourse on Christian higher education: Curry and Wells, *Faith Imagination in the Academy*; Dunaway, *Gladly Teach, Gladly Learn*; Henry and Beaty, *The Schooled Heart: Moral Formation in American Higher Education*; Hauerwas, *State of the University*; Houston et al., *Spirituality in Educational Leadership*; Jacobsen and Hustedt Jacobsen, *American University in a Postsecular Age*; Jeffrey and Evans, *Bible and the University*; Noll and Turner, *Future of Christian Learning*; Ortiz and Melleby, *Outrageous Idea of Academic Faithfulness*; Sommerville, *Decline of the Secular University*; Spears and Loomis, *Education for Human Flourishing*.

5. Hughes, *Models for Christian Higher Education*, 5–7.

6. Snell, "Making Men without Chests."

edge, would we not be abandoning an insight shared by all of Western culture since Aristotle—that knowledge is a good in itself, worth pursuing for its own sake? Would we not be abandoning the intellectualist view of man that came from Aristotle through Aquinas, to shape centuries of intellectualist humanism: that the highest good for man is truthful knowledge because, as Aristotle put it, "Man is *nous*—man is mind."[7]

Behind every pedagogy is an anthropology. What we think education does, what it is for, depends on our image of what we think humans do, what they are for, especially if we think that education should fit neatly with human capacity and structure, as most do. Our understanding of education, then, depends considerably on our definition of humanity. Monan articulates this as well, claiming that given the prevailing image of the human, "it would be difficult to overestimate the educational consequences of this simple expression of the philosophic nature of the human person and the identification of his highest good."[8] If, as he puts it, the "good life of a man or a woman is a life of mind," then that good defines the purpose and structures of university education almost entirely, emphasizing "those fields and those methodologies that will best fulfill the potentialities of mind."[9]

If the anthropology of mind is correct, then the resulting model of education is adequate, and certainly alive and well in practice. However, if this understanding is inadequate, then so too the education—and it is inadequate, the picture of the human as intellect is "a radical oversimplification of . . . the complexity of human nature and of its true good."[10] In a powerful description, Fr. Monan explains:

> I do not feel I need belabor the point that in Jewish and Christian biblical tradition, the measure of a man or a woman was never to be found in the magnitude of one's intellectual attainments. That measure was to be found rather in how sensitively, how responsively, one exercised his or her freedom. The great Commandment is: Thou shall love the Lord thy God with thy whole heart and mind and soul, and thy neighbor as thyself.

7. Monan, "Value Proposition."

8. Ibid.

9. Ibid.

10. Ibid.

A new "reference point" other than *knowledge* is required to "serve as magnetic 'north' in defining liberal education's purpose"[11]—and that magnetic north is *love*.

PERSONS AS LOVERS

Given the prevalence of the "thinking things" mindset, it is unsurprising that much of Christian higher education has concerned itself with worldview analysis—anthropology and pedagogy tend to follow and support each other. While not strictly coterminous with the integration model, the default position often linked worldview and integration closely, claiming that Christians, like all thinkers, bring unique foundational assumptions to their disciplines; consequently, Christian scholarship differs from its secular counterparts in its foundations.[12] In fact, so prevalent is worldview thinking that unease with it is partly responsible for the expanded conversation indicated previously.[13] As one of the leading voices pushing back against the thinking things model in favor of the lovers, James K. A. Smith opens his book *Desiring the Kingdom: Worship, Worldview, and Cultural Formation* by asking of the purpose of education, and what difference a Christian education makes, claiming that most often "education is about ideas and information . . . so distinctively *Christian* education is understood to be about Christian ideas . . . the development of a Christian perspective . . . worldview."[14] Smith goes beyond a typical answer, suggesting that the primary purpose of education, Christian or otherwise, is less about information and more about "*formation* of hearts and desires."[15] Using a variety of images to articulate this, he wonders if informing the intellect might be better recast as grabbing us by the gut, or shaping the heart, or transforming our imagination. Corralling the variety of images into a concise project, he suggests

11. Ibid.

12. Peterson and Snell indicate several representative texts in this vein; see for example Hamilton and Mathisen, "Faith and Learning at Wheaton College," 271; Sire, *Universe Next Door* and *Naming the Elephant*; and Dockery and Thornbury, *Shaping a Christian Worldview*. For a history of worldview thinking and its educational implications, see Naugle, *Worldview*.

13. Peterson and Snell identify Schwehn, *Exiles from Eden*; Solberg, *Lutheran Higher Education in North America*; Jacobsen and Jacobsen, *Scholarship and Christian Faith*; Hughes, *Vocation of a Christian Scholar*, esp. 42–68.

14. Smith, *Desiring the Kingdom*, 17.

15. Ibid., 18.

[handwritten: Modernism + language — we oversimplify ↑ — constantly]

[handwritten: Christ?] that education is not "first and foremost about what we know, but about what we love," and we entirely agree.[16]

When Smith argues for an education of the *gut*, he expresses concern about the usual way of conceiving higher education, including the status of embodiment for education, a desire to break the neat seals of the classroom to have education engage all of life, and a sophisticated account of cultural formation and the role of liturgy. But as interesting as he is on those matters, it is his philosophical anthropology which is of most interest here, for as he suggests, "behind every pedagogy is a philosophical anthropology" and "Christian education has absorbed a philosophical anthropology that sees human persons as primarily thinking things."[17] Consequently, Christian education has devoted considerable effort and attention to "the dissemination and communication of Christian ideas" or worldview, primarily understood as a system of beliefs, as an "epistemic framework," beginning always with the primacy of mind.[18]

Smith suggests an alternative model rooted in the primacy of love because humans are "first and foremost: loving, desiring, affective, liturgical animals who, for the most part, don't inhabit the world as thinkers or cognitive machines."[19] In fact, a good deal of our involvement or engagement in the world is pre-cognitive, pre-theoretical, and pre-reflective—although this is *not* to suggest unintelligent or irrational. Humans may in fact be rational animals, but this is not to suggest that we start our engagement with the world from a position of ideas, abstractions, or beliefs. Instead, we start with a stance, a way of being in the world revealing our projects and intentions, our cares and concerns. This is not to imply that ideas have no consequences, but ideas emerge from a stance and way of approaching the world, the way we *love* or care.

In some ways, this is a deceptively simple claim: if we did not approach the world with certain concerns and intentions nothing would emerge in consciousness worth attention. Ideas, hypotheses, insights, doctrines, systems of belief, all arise in consciousness because we care enough to advert to the world, and the way we advert to the world shapes the various ways the world appears, the way it is *for us*.

16. Ibid.
17. Ibid., 31.
18. Ibid.
19. Ibid., 34.

In formulating his anthropology, Smith hopes to pivot education towards worship, claiming that we are *homo liturgicus*, worshipping beings, with cultural and social practices forming our identities. With just a tint of antithesis about his project, he critiques the cultural liturgies of our society and suggests alternative practices and liturgies more adequate to the formation of people for the kingdom. In one very helpful section of the text, he suggests that grasping his alternative model of the person as lover requires understanding a nexus of related concepts and terms: (1) intentionality, or love's aim; (2) teleology, or love's end; (3) habits, or love's fulcrum; and (4) practices, or love's formation.[20] Our project is not opposed to his, but it is somewhat narrower, we "hunker down" on the first of his concepts, intentionality, trying to unveil the richness and fecundity of the notion.

INTENTIONALITY AND THE ENGAGEMENT OF LOVE

It may seem counter-intuitive to claim that a narrowed focus on intentionality is supportive rather than inimical to the project of critiquing the "thinking things" model. After all, intentionality, as we consider it, is largely a philosophy of consciousness, a phenomenology of subjectivity, and we ground a good deal of our argument in the structures and transcendental precepts of a turn to the human subject. We will not devote much attention to worship, cultural practices, conditions of social life, or embodiment. This is not, however, hostility or oversight of those realities, but rather a close read of what it means to be conscious lovers. To be sure, our project can, and should, be supplemented by the sort of reflections Smith and others provide, just as we claim that our project can be thought of as a supplement or sustained deliberation about one aspect of his. Naturally, we think we offer something of value.

The turn to subjectivity is somewhat out of favor these days, even viewed with obvious suspicion by the very proponents of an anthropology of love.[21] Historicity, language, and embodiment are supposedly indicative of what happens when the turn to the subject is left behind, or at least minimized, with too much concern for subjectivity supposedly indicating entrenchment in the Cartesian trap of the inner space

---

20. Ibid., 47–63.

21. For an especially interesting text, see Kanaris and Doorley, *In Deference to the Other*, especially the Foreword by Jack Caputo.

of the mind. Those concerns are justified if the turn to the subject is not performed properly, if intentionality analysis is thought something like an inner-looking or privileged gaze at oneself. If, however, the turn to the subject is performed well, those concerns can be avoided and a normative grasp of authentic subjectivity—what we term *authentic cosmopolitanism*—attained and defended in a mode entirely conversant with historicity, temporality, language, sociality, and embodiment, what we later term the *hermeneutics of facticity*.[22] All that remains to be articulated, but we are not ignorant of those concerns and possible objections. For the moment, we can do no more than to insist that ours is an anthropology rooted in love, in the engaged agency of concrete (i.e., historical and actual) human beings, and explain more in the following pages. For the moment, consider intentionality.

Smith suggests that his model starts from "an *intentional* account of human persons."[23] Rather than assuming the Cartesian divide between ideas and the extra-mental world, with a corresponding notion of the mind as a kind of inner space for ideas, intentionality analysis considers the human as always already involved with the world, always intending or aiming at the world as an object of consciousness. Consciousness is always intentional, always aimed and involved, such that the Cartesian idea of the "thinking thing" is obviously truncated—thought is always "about" or "of" something, never just "thought" or "thinking" in inner space.[24]

If intentionality meant only object-ification, it might be construed as remaining within the thinking thing model, but intentionality has more flesh than simply thinking about something, for we always intend the world in some particular mode. Intentionality is inhabited, involved, engaged. Humans approach the world and its myriad objects in some way of involvement, under some guise—as bored, or indifferent, or delighted, or afraid, or nostalgic, or curious—and the same extra-mental object exists for us in a variety of different ways. We approach reality with a certain comportment, what Heidegger calls "care" or "concern," or Augustine calls "love," or what Charles Taylor or Lonergan will discuss as "value," and the world changes as a result.

22. Lawrence, "Expanding Challenge to Authenticity in *Insight*," 427–56.
23. Smith, *Desiring the Kingdom*, 47.
24. Ibid., 48.

Intentional existence is always concrete, always the way of being of a particular person at a particular time; consequently, consciousness is not itself an abstract or reified thing, and while we can arrive at universal structures and claims about consciousness which are true, normative, and invariant for all persons, these structures are known only through the self-knowledge and appropriation of concrete persons. Eric Voegelin explains:

> Human consciousness is not a free-floating something but always the concrete consciousness of concrete persons ... for consciousness is always concretely founded on man's bodily existence, through which he belongs to all levels of being, from the anorganic to the animalic. . . . Concrete man orders his existence from the level of his consciousness, but that which is to be ordered is not only his consciousness but his entire existence in the world.[25]

A study of consciousness, thus, properly understood, is a study of the whole human, in all their pursuits and engagements and involvements of their existence, as well as the entire world of meaning and action with which they are involved. Intentionality is a study of all the ways we love, and all the things loved, and a thorough understanding of love is to already understand, in a limited way, all that there is to love.

Still, consciousness is known only by knowing oneself; there is no such thing as "Consciousness" to be studied, no "Intentionality" to be analyzed. There is just the concrete, existing human person in their embodied individuality, sociality, historicity, and temporality. Consciousness is always placed. And a study of consciousness is a study of the existing person, with all their authenticity and inauthenticity, intelligence and stupidity, transcendence and wickedness. As a result, to understand love as it should be we turn to the converted subject, the authentic person.

THE CONVERTED SUBJECT

Coming to terms with the whole existence of a concrete subject is to come across the joker in the deck of education, for persons are not always authentic, rational, or virtuous; in fact, the doctrine of original sin would suggest that the greatest impediment to education is not igno-

25. Voegelin, *Anamnesis*, 200.

Sin spoken of in generalities

rance but the existential disorder of sinfulness. Oddly, despite the doctrine of original sin and the so-called noetic effects of the Fall, concrete and detailed discussion of its implications for education are quite rare.[26] Many texts never mention sin in their account of education, even when it is assumed and polemically used against theological positions deemed overly optimistic—an odd failure to link theology to educational philosophy.[27] Even when discussed, the tendency is towards a vague abstraction, for example, "reason is partly debilitated . . . and we grope our way through various errors . . . there remains some desire to learn, some clarity of mind, some love of truth."[28] More sophisticated accounts will usually include reference to a narrative of Creation-Fall-Redemption, but the nod is fairly limited and often a generality without much implication for the actual pedagogy.[29]

Even when sin is discussed, the account is often truncated, with serious oversights, as argued by Stephen Moroney.[30] First, the tradition tends to suppose that sin impairs our ability to know God much more than knowledge in the sciences and liberal arts; religious knowledge is hurt, but secular knowledge escapes relatively unimpaired. Second, very often the antithesis between the redeemed and the unbeliever is made so strongly that the limits of noetic sin seem all but overcome for the believer, especially if they have a proper worldview with a place for everything and everything in its place. Third, the consequences are often considered in oddly asocial ways, as if sin affected only individuals and not social structures and institutions, or as if social sin is mainly about moral and religious truth—think of certain culture war depictions of the disingenuous scientist or cultural elite. Fourth, the reality of grace and redemption tends to be discussed in the most abstract manner, as if grace did not operate within the structures of concrete human sub-

26. See Moroney, *Noetic Effects of Sin*, as well as Moroney, "How Sin Affects Scholarship," 432–51. For a helpful summary and engagement with Moroney see Hoitenga, "Noetic Effects of Sin," 68–102.

27. For examples of influential texts without *any* apparent place for sin in education, see Holmes's *Idea of a Christian College*, Hughes, *Vocation of a Christian Scholar*, and Litfin, *Conceiving the Christian College*. For examples of polemical use against Thomas Aquinas, and a response, see Snell, "Thomism and Noetic Sin, Transposed," 7–28.

28. Holmes, *Building the Christian Academy*, 67.

29. For example, see the influential and substantial book by Wolters, *Creation Regained*.

30. See Moroney, *Noetic Effects of Sin*.

jectivity. To be sure, there are some thinkers doing sophisticated work on these issues, but their insights have not as yet permeated the default position.[31]

We suggest these oversights occur because of the relationship between anthropology and pedagogy. It is perfectly coherent for the default position to think of sin as a conceptual category within the puzzle-piece nexus of concepts making up the system. Coherent, but truncated, lacking the methodological resources for an anthropology of the concrete existential subject.[32] Our own method begins with the existing subject: "it is the study of oneself inasmuch as one is conscious . . . attends to operations and to their center and source which is the self."[33] By attending to the concrete operations of the self, we avoid the thinking thing truncation, just as we avoid a conceptualist abstraction about sin and grace, for sin and grace are apparent in the operations and acts of consciousness. The disorders of sin and the restorations of grace are real and actual and knowable in our own selves, and since we are primarily lovers the concreteness of sin and grace is in the order and disorder of love. The *ordo amoris* is the heart of education.

We have no particular objection to information, systems of belief, or worldview analysis as having a proper place in education, for of course ideas and systems matter and must be done properly; we do hesitate to make those functions the foundation and purpose of education, especially an education of concrete persons and their loves, especially an education of persons with disordered and sinful loves, finding ourselves in agreement with Greg Clark's depiction of the default model's truncated understanding of love's conversion:

> Conversion in worldview philosophy culminates in gaining admission to a theater of worldviews. When one converts to Jesus, one has a sense that nothing is more real than this One who wrecked the gates of hell, whereas in worldview philosophy one is keenly aware of the distance between one's worldview and reality. Coming into contact with Jesus inspires worship . . . while

---

31. For examples of more sophisticated thinkers on these issues, see Plantinga, *Warranted Christian Belief*, 199–240; Griffiths, *Intellectual Appetite*; Westphal, *Overcoming Onto-theology*; Wolterstorff, *Educating for Shalom*.

32. See Lonergan, "Subject," 420–35.

33. Ibid., 424.

worldview philosophy brings us out of dogmatism but has tendencies towards skepticism.[34]

It is telling that Clark utilizes a pagan, Plato, to criticize the lack of conversion in Christian models of education, arguing that the cave analogy of the *Republic* "offers us a picture of the movement in the spiritual life of the philosopher . . . a process of continual education, transformation and conversion."[35] As opposed to the default position "the language of conversion makes it clearer . . . that one's life is at stake, not just one's beliefs or presuppositions. To use the Platonic imagery, one does not emerge from the cave as an eyeball; the entire body must ascend. Conversion requires that our desires—our loves and our hates—change."[36]

Since we wish to provide a foundation for education in a phenomenology of the concrete existing subject, and since we think this reveals the subject to exist as a lover, and since the reality of sin disorders loves concretely, our understanding of education centers on the conversions of love. We differentiate between intellectual, moral, and religious conversion, arguing for the role of each in a full-orbed pedagogical vision, and arguing that a proper study of the human subject—their loves and conversions—allows for a robust and normative understanding of *authenticity*, a notion we link to Lonergan's description of *cosmopolis*.

A FINAL WORD

In the following pages thinkers of diverse backgrounds and vocabularies are placed in conversation with each other—Plato, Augustine, Aquinas, Heidegger, Taylor, Scheler, for example—but the unifying theme in all is the notion that humans are not disengaged minds but engaged lovers, with thought operating as one mode of love. The major influence for the text is the Jesuit theologian-philosopher Bernard Lonergan, our account of intentionality largely his, and our readings of other thinkers like Augustine and Aquinas influenced by that account. It is our assumption that Lonergan is not necessarily well known, or at least little evidence exists that his thought is utilized in the conversations on Christian education, and we view this as a brief introduction to his work as well as an account of intentionality and engaged subjectivity. Our focus is

34. Clark, "Nature of Conversion," 217.

35. Ibid., 211–12.

36. Ibid., 218.

on intentionality and its teleology, love and the implications for human flourishing, rather than any direct application for university study, although certainly such applications could be made—but first things first, and so we turn to love.

PART ONE

The Order of Authentic Love and Intellectual Conversion

1

Noetic Exegesis and the Authentic Intellect

In this chapter we suggest that Plato, Augustine, and Aquinas assist an anthropology of love, especially in developing a noetic exegesis of interiority. To put it another way, all three thinkers, each in their own way and with varying levels of sophistication, turn inward, studying and objectifying their own conscious operations by which they know and act, only to discover the primacy of love. We consider Plato's account of education by which one's loves are formed, Augustine's struggle in the *Confessions* to explicate an account of knowing not limited to matter, his theoretical advances in *De Trinitate*, and Aquinas' appropriation of the active intellect.

For understandable reasons, the argument and sources used are not the usual ones in contemporary reflection on Christian higher education, certainly not in the evangelical Protestant world. One could hardly begrudge the default model for overlooking Charles Taylor, Martin Heidegger, or Bernard Lonergan as they write from traditions somewhat different than the default model, but a more serious gap likely exists in our use of Plato, Augustine, and Aquinas. At the heart of both Roman Catholic and Protestant traditions, Augustine is strongly represented in the conversation, Reformed or otherwise, but the elements of Augustine highlighted here, the intellectual conversion of the *Confessions* and the psychological analogy of *De Trinitate*, are generally not utilized or actively criticized as mistaken.[1] Plato and Aquinas fare quite poorly in the literature, more often used as foils and bogeymen than helpful models, at least in part because of the default position's dependence on neo-cal-

---

1. The psychological analogy has fallen on hard times, for one widely influential example, see Gunton, "Augustine, The Trinity and the Theological Crisis of the West," 33–58.

vinism, a tradition often opposed to Plato and Aquinas. James Smith, for example, with whom we share a conception of the anthropology of love, uses the common narrative, albeit in a sophisticated version, lumping Plato with Descartes' anthropology of the "thinking thing," antipathy to the body, and deeply unchristian account of the created realm.[2] As for Aquinas, he comes off terribly, supposedly creating a zone for reason autonomous from, and at potentially at odds with, revelation, and with a semi-Pelagian optimism concerning reason.[3]

Of course, we do not intend to claim that Plato was a proto-Christian or that Augustine and Aquinas are never mistaken or do not borrow (too) heavily from pagan thought, but they are masters of interiority, and if we are concerned primarily with the formation of love it makes sense to re-read these thinkers. Granted, they operate within the limits of their times, but each makes significant contributions to understanding those operations by which humans know and act, thus allowing for a creative retrieval of their thought deeply in keeping with more contemporary understandings of subjectivity.

PLATO AND THE THERAPY OF DESIRE

With respect to education and love, Plato knows few betters, if read properly. Often reading with an eye to his conceptual apparatus, many people think of "Platonism" when they think of Plato—Forms, recollection, participation, the Good, and the tripartite soul. If, however, we consider the dialogues less like inefficient essays and more like existential drama, we see that the "doctrines" of Platonism could profitably be understood as symbols of order around which individuals and communities could reorient their loves and move from existential revolt to order.[4] The dialogues allow readers and disciples to encounter the order of the inner polis and a noetic interpretation of their own consciousness,

---

2. Smith, *Desiring the Kingdom*, 41; *Introducing Radical Orthodoxy*, 197–206.

3. For discussion on Aquinas and his reception, see Snell, "Thomism and Noetic Sin," and also Dooyeweerd, *In the Twilight of Western Thought*, 40–44; Schaeffer, *Escape from Reason*, 9–42; Schaeffer, *How Should We Then Live*; Pearcey, *Total Truth*, 74–95; Walsh and Middleton, *Transforming Vision*, 98–116; Goheen and Bartholomew, *Living at the Crossroads*; Seerveld, *Christian Critique of Art and Literature*; Vos, *Aquinas, Calvin, and Contemporary Protestant Thought*.

4. Voegelin, *Plato*, 5–6.

even if, admittedly, Plato never raises the notion of noetic interpretation in an explicitly methodical way.

Eric Voegelin provides a creative retrieval of Plato where a noetic interpretation of consciousness is central, "traced back to its origin in the consciousness of men who desire true knowledge of order. The consciousness of concrete men is the place where order is experienced."[5] The primary experience of order is that of wonder, the simultaneous recognition of one's ignorance and the pull towards the luminosity of the real. Having experienced in one's own self the pull of wonder, "noetic interpretations arise when consciousness . . . seeks to become explicit to itself," and since the making explicit of one's own conscious experience is "not blind desire but rather contains the component of insight, we may characterize it as knowing questioning and questioning knowledge."[6] Such exegesis objectifies concrete consciousness, from within, but not as an "Archimedean point" from which to view consciousness "itself as an object."[7] That is, while the conscious experience of order can be adverted to as an "object" of study, consciousness can never be made an "object" of study from afar, as if consciousness was able to separate itself from itself to take a good long look in pure perception; instead, consciousness is caught up into the reflexive study of itself, unable to view itself from afar.

Consequently, when the response to wonder "becomes luminous to itself . . . and when the question becomes an act of reflective questioning," it is possible to derive a "record of such experiences" breaking "forth into self-exegesis by means of language symbols."[8] However, in Voegelin's understanding of philosophers, of whom Plato is paramount, the language symbols are not to be read as reified entities or hypostatized constructions, for such "distort the reality that we want to explore."[9] Philosophers of order experience the pull of conscious intentionality towards reality and understand that intentionality well enough to create symbols of the experience to "imaginatively recreate the engendering experience and . . . articulate the truth of order . . . to restore public consciousness of the engendering experiences so that they will

5. Voegelin, *Anamnesis*, 147.

6. Ibid., 148.

7. Ibid., 153.

8. Voegelin, "Beginning and the Beyond," 173, 178.

9. Ibid., 179.

have an ordering effect on individuals and society."[10] Philosophy is more poetic than doctrinaire, and reading ancient philosophers as if they are presenting us with a philosophical system misunderstands philosophy. Moreover, it distorts personal reality and misses out on philosophic education—*paideia*—which forms order instead of existential revolt.

The Socratic character is a symbol through which Plato hopes to communicate the order founded by the person of Socrates, with the dialogue the means for presenting the symbol.[11] The trial of Socrates reveals the disorder of Athens and Plato's awareness that justice is unlikely to be found through politics. Athens is put on trial, and Athens is guilty, but hope remains in the conversion to philosophic friendship and community of the city's best young men. The young are converted through conversation, as evidenced by Socrates' refusal to engage in oratory and threats to leave if the harangue of an orator supplants dialogue. In the *Apology* and *Symposium*, for instance, Socrates is expected to deliver a speech but instead convinces (and thus convicts) his accuser, Meletus, or competition, Agathon, to allow the cross examination of their position instead. In the *Republic*, Cephalus, the lover of speeches, is driven off so Socrates can engage his son, Polemarchus, in conversation, and Thrasymachus is forced into question and answer, dooming his sophistry. In *Protagoras* and *Gorgias* inveterate speechmakers hesitantly allow discussion as friends—each finds, in some small way, their internal order becoming like Socrates'.

These episodes reveal the Socratic commitment to midwifery, for since wisdom and virtue cannot be taught, the main task of the dialogic form is to create existential community modeled after Socrates' own existential order. Dialogue is the means by which the interlocutor imitates Socrates, a lover, a philosopher, as Pierre Hadot explains:

> philosophy no longer meant, as the Sophists had it, acquiring knowledge, know-how, or *Sophia*; it meant questioning ourselves, because we have the feeling that we are not what we ought to be . . . this feeling comes from the fact that, in the person of Socrates, we have encountered a personality which, by its mere presence, obliges those who approach it to question them-

10. Federici, *Eric Voegelin*, 136–39.
11. Ibid., 10.

selves . . . Socrates acts upon his listeners in an irrational way, by the emotions he provokes and the love he inspires.[12]

Having concluded that Athens was incorrigibly corrupt and that virtue could not simply be taught in speech, Plato suggests a new, ordered polis—a community in common search for wisdom. So it should serve as no surprise that the informal conversation of Socrates is transformed into the Academy of Plato, nor surprising that Plato had his own missionary journeys to found such communities; philosophy "could be carried out only by means of a community of life and dialogue between masters and disciples, within the framework of a school."[13] The school itself has a kind of "sacramental character," for the force of ordered reason becomes "incarnate in the community of the erotic souls as in its mystical body."[14]

The community of souls is the *sine qua non* of Socratic philosophy, for the community goes well beyond the written word; what is taught is not "put down on paper as a teachable doctrine," but rather "to be read and re-read in communion."[15] Pierre Hadot argues that in the schools of antiquity the written text serves two functions, one to express the school's "vision of the world, its own style of life, and its idea of the perfect man" in a kind of public apologetic for the school, and second, as an introduction of the school to new converts. Note, however, that the practice of philosophy was not identified with the writing and discussion of systematic treatises, with the ideas—"to philosophize is to choose a school, convert to its way of life, and accept its dogmas." While theory is certainly not absent from the philosophical life, it is not primary:[16]

> . . . philosophy did not consist in teaching an abstract theory—much less in the exegesis of texts—but rather in the art of living. It is a concrete attitude and determinate lifestyle, which engages the whole of existence. The philosophical act is not situated merely on the cognitive level, but on that of the self and of being. It is a progress which causes us to *be* more fully, and make us better. It is a conversion which turns our entire life upside down, changing the life of the person who goes through it. It raises the individual

12. Hadot, *What is Ancient Philosophy?*, 29–30.

13. Ibid., 56.

14. Voegelin, *Plato*, 18.

15. Ibid., 19, 23.

16. Hadot, *Philosophy as a Way of Life*, 57, 60.

from an inauthentic condition of life, darkened by unconscious-
ness and harassed by worry, to an authentic state of life. . . . [17]

The philosophical *act*, the operation of philosophy, was engaged to convert its practitioners from inauthenticity to authenticity, from disorder
to order—it was an education of desire.

Plato makes this clear in the *Republic*, detailing his conception of
desire's education, particularly if the text concerns the existential ordering of the inner polis of soul rather than a prescription for an ideal city-
state. Very often the text is read not as a treatise on education, which it
explicitly purports to be, but as political or metaphysical treatise, and
for some good reasons. Yet Plato himself suggests otherwise. First, the
defense of justice in Book II, where the argument really begins, Book I
having ended in aporia, is occasioned because of the bad education on
justice provided to the young by their fathers, the poets, and the customs
of the city, each teaching that justice is undesirable in itself but sought
for its benefits.[18] Second, the ideal city of speech, the kallipolis, is a technique chosen because helpful in finding justice in the soul, but the just
soul is the goal of the inquiry.[19] Third, that point is emphasized again
in Book V when Socrates declares that the city was constructed as an
ideal type with which to criticize actual constitutions, but that he should
not be compelled to demonstrate how the kallipolis could actually come
into existence, as this was not the point: "we weren't trying to discover
these things in order to prove that it's possible for them to come into
being."[20] He insists, as well, that practice never matches up to theory and
that improving an actual city should happen through as few and small
changes as possible, quite unlike the perfect city's purges and marriages.[21]
Fourth, the link between the education of the guardians and the images
of education given in the Sun, Line, and Cave is often neglected, but
the three images are sandwiched between discussions of education—the
finale of the guardians and the advent of the philosophers—and Socrates
insists that the cave is "an image of our nature in its education and want
of education."[22]

17. Ibid., 83.
18. Plato, 363a–367c.
19. Ibid., 369a.
20. Ibid., 472d.
21. Ibid., 472a–473c.
22. Ibid., 514a.

The prisoners are bound, viewing only shadows cast by others behind them. Once loosed, they timorously ascend from the world of images to things, hypotheticals, Forms, and finally to the Sun-Good. The task of the philosopher's education is apparent, for dialectical education moves the soul to knowledge of what is, but the fundamental problem posed by the Cave is just how the prisoners are freed. The philosopher's education is provided only to those who have already passed a battery of intellectual and character tests, thus already freed, and so philosophical education is not the means of freeing the prisoners but given only to those already outside the cave. Plato is quite adamant about this, for the dangers of creating a false philosopher are simply too great to give to the imprisoned. So how, then, are the prisoners to be freed? The text suggests the prisoner is released and turns (*periagoge*) away from the shadow world, they convert.[23] The conversion is not by dialectics but rather through the education of desire cultivated through the moral education of the guardians.

Given Plato's concern with the formation of love, it should not surprise us that the Republic begins with a concern not about the philosopher

> but rather about moral imagination. A just education begins with fiction, with fairy tales about gods and heroes and noble men so as to educate taste, to educate a love of what is noble but disgust and shame about what is ignoble. This is an education of the moral imagination, for in stories are these tastes formed, and in tastes the loves, what is valued, and what is valued will sustain much longer, and much deeper, than what is merely believed.[24]

In the early books, Socrates examines the pleasures of the guardians, both proper and improper. Guardians are educated to not feel pain at death, to not covet material goods, and to avoid licentiousness and gluttony. Education of pleasure is, as Socrates remarks, an indelible dye in "opinion about what is terrible and what is not."[25]

Education in desire matters because whatever is thought most pleasant is also considered the "plainest and truest reality," for whatever we care about dominates our attention.[26] It is for this reason that the

23. Ibid., 518c.
24. Snell, "Men without Chests."
25. Plato, *Republic*, 429e–430b.
26. Plato, *Phaedo*, 83c.

prisoners in the cave take so much delight in their captivity, even award-
ing honor to those best equipped at existence in this shadow world, and
finding their salvation so discomforting.[27] The guardians, however, have
been habituated to feel only shame at lower pleasures. The anthropo-
morphic gods and incontinent heroes of the poets are replaced with
rational and ordinate perfections, and the guardians' appetites are mod-
erated, their spirit controlled and directed, with lapses into extremes of
emotion limited through the control of music, poetry, and gymnastic.
Furthermore, the guardians are given a taste for permanence, for what
does not change. They love order but hate innovation in law and education, their theology centers on the good and unchanging gods whom
they emulate, and so when it comes time to confront the unchanging
Forms they discover what they already loved. The guardians are trained
by their delights to be those most capable of philosophy, and are those
that escape the cave, all because of an education in desire:

> In such an atmosphere [the guardians] will acquire not only a
> natural grace and proportion of bearing and character, but an
> instinctive sense of what is fair and what is foul in nature and in
> art; and this instinctive sense is a kind of anticipation of a ratio-
> nal understanding of the nature of good and evil; for the reason
> which is now presented to them in forms of sense, and calls forth
> sensuous delight, is the same reason which they will afterwards
> learn to know in its own form as an intelligible principle, and
> which they will then recognize as an old friend with a new face.[28]

Recall that Plato is concerned with existential order in response to
the disorder of Athens, and he responds through conversation, in part
through the construction of the perfect city in speech. Conversation exists to form good souls, and thus, at the end of Book IX Socrates can
claim "it's better for all to be ruled by what is divine and prudent, especially when one has it as his own within himself," and that a wise person
cares for "the regime within him," for "his own city."[29] The *Republic*,
then, concerns the inner regime and the best way to manage the soul.

Despite the disorder of Athens, Plato turns away from politics and
forms schools, where the point of the Academy was not exegesis of texts
but conversation and formation; texts were means to experience the in-

27. Plato, *Republic*, 516c,d; *Phaedo* 82e–83e.
28. Nettleship, *Theory of Education in Plato*, 62.
29. Plato, *Republic*, 590d; 591d,e; 592a.

ner city of Socrates and repeat this in one's own soul. Disciples were trained in desires and then dialectic, which is exactly what happens in the *Republic*. This inner turn is *done* as a discipline much more than is thematized as a method—doing before knowing—but Voegelin provides a creative retrieval and thematization in light of later developments in philosophy. One of those later developments is Augustine, something of a Platonist, but it is no accident that his own inner turn is in keeping with the Platonic turn, even if Augustine explicitly thematizes this in a way not yet possible for Plato.

AUGUSTINE AND INTELLECTUAL CONVERSION

In recent years "Augustine has become the whipping boy of much modern Trinitarian theology," Neil Ormerod claims, and "it is not uncommon to find slated home to his writings on the Trinity, specifically *De Trinitate*, all that is wrong with western Trinitarian theology."[30] The reasons given for the suspicion are varied, with some critics accepting a basic typology between the theological traditions of the Christian West and East, apparently divided between the Western concern for unity and the Eastern concern with plurality and communion. Over-emphasizing unity risks modalism, reduces the *ad extra* work of economic Trinity into the work of the unity, creates the conditions for modern individualism, and is thus responsible for a host of epistemological, political, and ontological absurdities.[31]

A clear issue concerns Augustine's responsibility for the invention of the modern self. One intellectual history suggests that Augustine is a proto-Cartesian, turning inwards to the self, perhaps even concocting the notion of an inner space or self to which we have immediate and privileged access, knowledge of which is the refutation of skepticism.[32] As the widely influential Charles Taylor would have it, Plato and Descartes are cousins in their conception of the self, and "on the way" between them "stands Augustine."[33] This modern self becomes its own autonomous standard for desire, and eventually liberates itself from a

---

30. Ormerod, "Augustine and the Trinity: Whose Crisis?," 17.

31. See Gunton, "Theological Crisis"; Ormerod, *Trinity: Retrieving the Western Tradition*; Drilling, "Psychological Analogy of the Trinity," 320–37.

32. For a thorough exposition of Augustine and inwardness, see the three volumes by Cary, *Augustine's Invention of the Inner Self*; *Inner Grace*; and *Outward Signs*.

33. Taylor, *Sources of the Self*, 127.

thick, charged world of meaning and order, now free to do as it wishes governed by not much more than its own self-interest.[34]

We're not especially interested in narrating (or defending) Augustine in relation to modernity, but we do claim that his famous inward turn allows for a sophisticated account of knowing whereby love is given priority, evidenced most particularly in the intellectual conversion of the *Confessions* and *De Trinitate*, and, moreover, that the inward turn assumes a method akin to Plato's noetic exegesis of the concrete subject, thus providing a critically grounded introspection rather than a merely abstract anthropology of love.

Ulcerous Corporeality[35]

In the *Confessions*, Augustine powerfully describes the condition in which he begins his studies at Carthage: "all around me in my ears were the sizzling and frying of unholy loves. I was not yet in love, but I loved the ideas of love . . . Being in love with love I looked for something to love."[36] Disordered, he had no desire for the incorruptible or abiding, but his sick soul "burst into fever spots which brought the wretched longing to be scratched by contact with the objects of sense."[37] Or, as one translator puts it, "in an ulcerous condition it thrust itself to outward things. . . ."[38]

Augustine recounts the many ways of his outward thrust, including the theatre, emotion, lust, the Wreckers, but then he reads the *Hortensius* of Cicero, a book which "changed my feelings. It altered my prayers, Lord, to be towards you yourself. It gave me different values and priorities. Suddenly every vain hope became empty to me, and I longed for the immortality of wisdom with an incredible ardour in my heart. I began to rise up to return to you."[39] He begins to leave the ulcerous condition, burning "with longing to leave earthly things and fly back to you."[40] He

---

34. For discussion, see Hanby, *Augustine and Modernity*, 6–26.

35. A similar argument on intellectual conversion is made in truncated form in Snell, "Teaching for Cosmopolis."

36. Augustine, *Confessions*, 3.1.

37. Ibid.

38. This is the translation of Chadwick, *Confessions*. Unless otherwise noted, quotations are from Chadwick's translation.

39. Ibid., 3.4.

40. Ibid.

cannot, however, appreciate the simplicity of Scripture and falls in with the Manicheans, rejecting the goodness of the physical order. In these sections Augustine returns again and again to the subject of physical images, giving multiple examples of objects sensed and imagined and begins a lengthy quest to overcome corporeal thinking. The main challenge is his conception of God, whom he considers a body, because he had not "followed the intelligence of the mind . . . but the mind of the flesh . . . living outside [himself], seeing only with the eye of the flesh."[41]

Nonetheless, he has "become to [himself] a vast problem" and begins to question his own soul, in part due to the death of a friend, a death causing despair but also awareness that physical objects and persons are reflective of a greater good.[42] Still he confesses that his "mind moved within the confines of corporeal forms," and continues to reduce spiritual realities to the physical, it is "miserable folly."[43] He hints that he might turn to examine the nature of the mind, but corporeal thinking interferes and he could not "see [his] mind;" he can use his intelligence but does not yet know what it is.[44]

Examining the mind, he doubts the Manichean sage Faustus, but takes pains to indicate that he still thinks of God as physical substance; when thinking of God he "knew of no way of doing so except as a physical mass. Nor did I think anything existed which is not material. *That was the principal and almost sole cause of my inevitable error.*"[45] The text is almost irritating about this, making the point frequently.

He loses all hope that truth can be found, just after he enters the Church no less, but he is "intent on inquiry and restless for debate," then immediately counters this enthusiasm by claiming that he has "not the least notion or even an obscure suspicion how there could be spiritual substance."[46] Even though his heart "vehemently protested against all the physical images in my mind," he fails, for "hardly had they been dispersed when in the flash of an eye they had regrouped and were back again. They attacked my power of vision and clouded it."[47] He grasps

41. Ibid., 3.6.
42. Ibid. 4.4.
43. Ibid., 4.15.
44. Ibid.
45. Ibid., 5.10, emphasis added.
46. Ibid., 6.3.
47. Ibid., 7.1.

conceptually that corporeality is inadequate, but to no avail, for he has not yet seen his mind: "my eyes are accustomed to such images. My heart accepted the same structure."[48] Moved by the desire to know, he almost overcomes the block, realizing "it was not in a place" that he thinks, but again the "inferior things came on top of me and pressed me down . . . they attacked me on all sides in massive heaps . . . the very images of physical objects formed an obstacle. . . . "[49] Until, at last, by God's grace, expressed here as unendurable "inward goads," Augustine discovers "through . . . inward perception" that God exists.[50] He enters his inner-most citadel and sees the light of God, he knows truth: "I would have found it easier to doubt whether I was myself alive that there is no truth 'understood from the things that are made.'"[51] He ascends from "bodies to the soul . . . and from there to its inward force . . . to the power of reasoning . . . it withdrew itself from the contradictory swarms of imaginative fantasies, so as to discover the light by which it was flooded."[52]

What happened in this somewhat exasperating journey? Augustine moved from a complete extroversion—that ulcerous condition—to an inner turn allowing him to acknowledge the reality of God, but this should not be read as if he turned inward and found God speaking to him in the recesses of his mind. God was not lurking about in Augustine waiting to be noticed; rather, in turning inward he discovers a reality—his own intellect—which was real and immaterial, thus allowing for the possibility that the category of real things need not be identified with the category of material things. This was a hard won reality, as even when he wants to believe in God he could not overcome the legacy of extroversion. Try as he might, the most familiar reality, the world of material bodies, retained its status as the standard of objective reality—the real must be the sort of thing that one could see, could image. The delay from wanting to believe to actually believing is made clear by his admission in Book III that he could not "see [his] mind," but once the mind was grasped in its immaterial operations the trap of extroversion was broken, and God could be acknowledged as having reality in a mode analogous to the mode of existence of his own mind. Real, but not material.

48. Ibid.
49. Ibid., 7.7.
50. Ibid., 7.8.
51. Ibid., 7.10.
52. Ibid., 7.17.

The *Confessions* reports this intellectual conversion, defined as an understanding that reality need not be modeled exclusively on the standards proper to extroversion. Another conception of the real emerges, made possible by the conversion. Still, this is much more of a report of what happened then it is an explanation. Some performance—conversion—has occurred, but the conditions of that performance are not yet thematized or made explicit as objects of study. Using language from Voegelin, Augustine has had a noetic experience but has not yet performed noetic exegesis, he has not "objectified" his own consciousness to discern the intentional operations *by which* he attained intellectual conversion. He's done the operations, and he has even reported that the operations made all the difference, but he has not yet pivoted his attention to study and identify them. He gets close to a noetic exegesis in Book X with its attention on memory, but even then there is a lack of clear differentiation, and it is always tempting to read his account of memory in those sections in a reified way, as if memory was a special faculty where God somehow *is* in some quasi-material way, a kind of ghostly materiality. In *De Trinitate*, however, with its famous and vilified psychological analogy, Augustine performs noetic exegesis. As Charles Taylor puts it, "Augustine shifts the focus from the field of objects known to the activity itself of knowing; God is to be found here," in a "reflexive stance" towards the acts of knowing themselves.[53] In reflexivity, our attention turns to a first-person standpoint where we "become aware of our awareness, try to experience our experiencing," and this reflexivity, noetic exegesis, is a major accomplishment of *De Trinitate*.[54]

Inward Is Upward: The Psychological Analogy

In addition to the objections to Augustine raised above, of all his supposed mistakes the psychological analogy is thought especially egregious, as Neil Ormerod explains:

> For over one thousand years the psychological analogy for the Trinity was the high point of Trinitarian theological reflection. From its origins in Augustine's *De Trinitate*, to its systematic exploitation in Aquinas' *Summa Theologiae*, and beyond in the myriad commentators on Aquinas, the analogy provided a focal organising principle for Western Trinitarian theology. Yet in

53. Taylor, *Sources*, 130.
54. Ibid.

the modern revival of Trinitarian thought, evident during the twentieth century, the analogy has been increasingly marginalized and even rejected by theologians in both the Protestant and Catholic traditions. It is now not uncommon to find dismissive comments about speculation on the "inner life of God" among theologians. . . . [55]

Against this, however, Ormerod articulates a counter-reading, one in which Augustine presents "a very precise phenomenology of human consciousness. . . ."[56] *De Trinitate* is organized in chiasm, with the early books discussing the Trinity from the vantage point of Scripture and theory, but with the pivotal moment occurring in Book 8, where Augustine declares " . . . let us turn our attention to the things we are going to discuss in a more inward manner than the things that have been discussed above, though in fact they are the same things," before examining interiority in several challenging books. [57] The turn inward is key, he claims, providing a "frame" for thinking around which to "weave what remains to be said" on the pattern of that frame.[58]

As one might expect, he warns that the biggest challenge to a proper understanding is corporeal thought, stating:

> it is easier and almost more familiar to deal with visible than with intelligible things, even though the former are outside and the latter inside us . . . we have grown so used to bodies, and our interest slips back and throws itself out into them . . . it runs away again to those things and seeks to take its ease in the place where it caught its disease."[59]

Instead, the inner turn requires adverting to a key experience, the insight into truth: "Come, hold it in that first moment in which so to speak you caught a flash from the corner of your eye when the word 'truth' was spoken . . . but you cannot; you slide back into these familiar and earthly things."[60] Despite the temptation of the body, the mind has access to itself: "What after all is so intimately known and so aware of its own

---

55. Ormerod, "Psychological Analogy for the Trinity," 281.

56. Ormerod, *Trinity*, 48.

57. Augustine, *Trinity*, 8.1. Hereafter *DT*.

58. *DT* 8.14.

59. Ibid., 11.1.

60. Ibid., 8.3.

existence as that by which things enter into our awareness, namely the mind?"[61]

Turning to the mind, he concentrates on the production of the inner word, which becomes the analogue to grasp the relationship of the Father and the Son, for while the knowledge of the Trinity is a matter of revelation, he is convinced that there should be some accessible analogue of three distinct realities which yet remain one, finding that human interiority, which always remains one, evidences three distinct operational realities, and all three operational realities are knowable through interior analysis.[62]

Knowing from the Gospel of John that God is love, Augustine stresses that while God is truth and goodness, above all God is love, and every expression of love hints at God by revealing a triadic structure of "the lover, what is being loved, and love."[63] However, instances of humans loving other humans are inadequate analogues since there are only two persons involved, not three, and the relations are not identical with either individual. The relation of the intellect to self-knowledge and self-love, however, appears more adequate. However, since the mind knows and the mind loves, it follows that there is one being with two activities, which is not adequate to the triune relations, a problem mitigated with a further analysis of the mind and the discovery of memory.

In knowing, the mind generates the verbum, "a kind of word that we beget by uttering inwardly, and that does not depart from us when it is born."[64] Note his striking claim that the word is born out of love, for the word is not generated unless there is a desire to know, inquisitiveness:

> This appetite, that is inquisitiveness, does not indeed appear to be the love with which what is known is loved . . . yet it is something of the same kind. It can already be called will because everyone who inquires wants to find out . . . everyone who inquires wants to know . . . parturition by the mind is preceded by a kind of appetite which prompts us to inquire and find out what we want to know, and as a result knowledge is conceived and brought forth as offspring.[65]

61. Ibid., 8.9.
62. Drilling, "Psychological Analogy," 323.
63. *DT* 8.14.
64. Ibid., 9.12.
65. Ibid., 9.18.

Consequently love precedes and follows the verbum—precedes as
the desire to know, follows as the willing of that which is known. For
Augustine, moreover, the truths which are known pursuant to inquiry
are not external to the mind, but are possessed in memory, and when the
desire to know emerges, the mind "comes out of itself in a kind of way
when it puts out feelings of love toward these images . . . imprinted on
the memory."[66]

We have a triadic account, for there is only one mind with three
distinct activities of memory, understanding, and love. Memory, as it
were, possesses truth, and when one desires to know this gives rise to
inquiry and the act of understanding, and, in turn, the will to love what
is known: "from its memory the mind generates knowledge of what it
remembers, and loves what it knows," and yet there is only one mind.[67]
The unity of the knowing/loving mind despite distinct operations
takes on particular significance when considering self-knowledge, for
if knowledge is generated from memory and love, and if we consider
self-knowledge an instance of knowledge generated in the same manner
as other types, then self-knowledge generates from the memory of self
already present to self—a striking instance of unity in the difference of
operations.

Of course, the turn inward leads us to this place, for Augustine
did not simply state that the turn would allow the formation of helpful conceptual apparatus, although he did and it does; he also *performs*
the inward turn when he inquires about his own mind, but to do so he
already had presence to self in memory to which he now attends and intends in the loving inquiry of his own self. Consequently, if "nothing can
be more present to [mind] than itself," there is a constant self-presence
requiring a form of introspection whereby the very same operations by
which *anything* is known are utilized to know operations themselves and
the self operating.[68]

Augustine differentiates his account of introspection from a naïve
version modeled on vision, whereby introspection is a kind of inner-
looking, almost as if the eye were able to bend around and look at itself, a
bizarre impossibility and out of keeping with the way knowledge is actually accrued, which is through loving inquiry and not staring: "You can-

66. Ibid., 10.11.
67. Drilling, "Psychological Analogy," 325.
68. *DT* 10.5; Ormerod, *Trinity*, 49.

not say the mind knows other minds and is ignorant of itself in the same sort of way as the bodily eye sees other eyes and does not see itself."[69] Rather than the naïve model, we know the mind when we perform, when we *do* what the mind does and then want (love) to know those very *doings*, but all this is possible only when we are thinking, when the activity is ongoing: "*whenever* we correctly approve or disapprove of something represented by such images, we have the inescapable conviction that we make our judgments of approval or disapproval within ourselves by altogether different rules which abide unchangeably above our minds."[70] Later he says we "make judgments about those things according to that form of truth, and we perceive that by insight of the rational mind,"[71] "observ[ing] with the eye of the mind the form . . . according to which we *do* anything with true and right reason."[72]

AQUINAS: THE HERMENEUTIC KEY

All thought occurs in historical situatedness, and Trinitarian reflections are no different. Medieval scholasticism, with Thomas Aquinas as a major figure, is no different, and yet his capacity to synthesize a variety of viewpoints into a new articulation makes him stand out as something of an originative genius, and also as a figure whose thought is particularly supple and forgiving of "creative retrieval." Consequently, it is unsurprising to find Thomistic revivals in the fourteenth century, early sixteenth, late nineteenth into the twentieth, and in our current time, just as each revival sees a proliferation of schools of interpretation, and their conflicts of interpretation, as well as opponents to the revival itself.[73]

Among other concerns, interpreters of Thomas in the century past grappled over how best to position him in relation to the modern turn to the subject, both in its early modern and later phenomenological modes.[74] One reason for the difficulty is that the theological achievements of the Scholastics emerged at a time when the Christian community moved into a new period of theoretical reflection, finding the former resources

69. Ibid., 9.3.

70. Ibid., 9.10, emphasis added.

71. Ibid., 9.11.

72. Ibid., 9.12.

73. See Cessario, *Short History of Thomism*.

74. An excellent history on the various schools of Thomism on this issue is McCool, *Neo-Thomists*.

of patristic and Augustinian thought not fully adequate to the need for understanding occasioned in their time.[75] Aristotle, especially as mediated by Islamic thought, proved helpful, and controversial, and even the brilliant synthesis accomplished by Aquinas was viewed with suspicion by some and rejected by others committed to the *via moderna*.

In our own time, the metaphysical commitments of Aquinas, heavily influenced by Aristotle, are still problematic. Aristotelian metaphysics and logic are spurned by some, the metaphysics of psyche and cognition are thought pre-critical and naïve to post-Kantian ears—let alone postmodern ears—and his Trinitarian thought is viewed with some suspicion, not only for his use and committed development of Augustine's psychological analogy, but for his own internal flaws as well. One influential objection is that because Thomas separates the discussion of God into two sections, one about the unity and simplicity of God, and the other an apparent afterthought about the Trinity, for resulting theologies as well as the faithful thereby influenced it could hardly matter at all if the doctrine of the Trinity were to be denied—nothing would change in our understanding of God.[76] A similar objection argues that the focus of the Trinity in God's own self devalues the economic Trinity as well as salvation history and revelation.[77] Third, Aquinas, like Augustine, over-privileges intellectualism and depends upon a faulty faculty psychology of intellect and rational will, but this comes at the expense of the credibility of love. Not only does this risk losing the theo-drama of God's salvific work, it risks losing the practical implications the Trinity might bring to bear on social and political concerns.[78]

We have no need to defend Augustine or Aquinas on these points, as our interest is not with the Trinity in itself but rather in the noetic exegesis discernable in the thinkers. We claimed earlier that we were less interested in *what* the philosophers said and more in *how* they said it, in their methodology. In Aquinas, like Plato and Augustine, we discern a rather sophisticated performance of the intellect and a move towards noetic exegesis useful for our anthropology of love.

An obvious difficulty in reading Aquinas in this manner is the apparent dependence on Aristotelian metaphysics; while he borrows

75. Tracy, *Achievement of Bernard Lonergan*, 45.

76. Kilby, "Aquinas, the Trinity and the Limits of Understanding," 415.

77. Ibid.

78. Hunt, *What are They Saying About the Trinity*, 62.

the analogy from Augustine, his articulation thereof, as indeed with much of his account of the soul and its intellectual operations, borrows heavily from Aristotle, with the consequence that he seems to develop a metaphysics of cognition dependant on a static, essentialistic faculty psychology. It is possible, however, to "develop a hermeneutic that could first expose the relevant psychological data and their epistemological implications before discussion of the involved metaphysical categories," or, to put it slightly differently, to turn to the "actual performance of Aquinas' own intellect."[79]

Clearly Aquinas is indebted to Aristotelian theory for his conceptual and linguistic apparatus, but as a subject his intelligence is not Aristotelian but human, and the performance of intellectual operations is pre-conceptual and pre-theoretical. The reading of Aquinas provided by Lonergan suggests that in working out the Trinitarian thought "Aquinas was engaged not merely in fitting an original Augustine creation into an Aristotelian framework but also in attempting, however remotely and implicitly, to fuse together . . . a phenomenology of the subject with a psychology of the soul."[80] This means that while the theoretical articulation is Aristotelian, the intelligence used to arrive at those concepts is adverted to, with the same "pivoting" of intelligence upon itself and its operations as found in Augustinian interiority.[81]

The result is a somewhat precarious balancing act. The very real limits of the Aristotelian metaphysics of cognition sometimes tend to overlook the very acts of understanding which are the source of the concepts, and consequently it is very easy to read Aristotle, and Aquinas, as if theirs are systems of concepts in relation to other concepts, with the whole game of thought exhausting itself in the puzzle-like manipulation and arrangement of those concepts, whether they relate to existence or not in any meaningful way—when grasp of the "intelligent generation of ideas is lost, it is not long before we are left without any real contact with the generative minds of our history."[82] Augustinian interiority tends to meliorate the risk of Aristotelian conceptualism, but in the end Augustine, so the argument goes, never fully overcomes his extroversion, merely refining it into a rarefied version with illumina-

---

79. Tracy, *Achievement of Bernard Lonergan*, 49–50.

80. Lonergan, *Verbum*, 3.

81. Tracy, *Achievement of Bernard Lonergan*, 51–52.

82. Ibid., 51.

tion the process whereby reality is known. Aristotle's own identity or adequational model of knowledge avoids any furtive attempts to slip-in extroversion as a model of knowledge, and so corrects the potentially naïve Augustinian account, just as Augustine corrects the potential conceptualism of Aristotle.[83] The result, according to Lonergan, is a phenomenology of the subject, rooted in a conscious pivoting towards the operations of intentionality, expressed in the language of a metaphysics of soul, with Aquinas' grasp of the psychological analogy grounded in his understanding of his own interiority, but expressed in a technically precise manner.

This is not to suggest that Aquinas knows Husserl, and Aquinas is limited and even at times distorted by the metaphysical constraints of his language, but it is to suggest that his conception of the inner word, *verbum*, at the heart of his Trinitarian understanding can itself be understood by a pivot to intelligence, by the noetic exegesis not only of Thomas' intellect but of our own.

Aquinas: Intelligible Emanation

It is undeniable that Aquinas' Trinitarian exposition occurs after his discussion of God, both in the *Summa's* order of exposition and in the logic of explanation. Very early in the text Aquinas indicates the priority of unity, for already in I 3 the notion of divine simplicity, or lack of composition, is made, and largely in Aristotelian terminology, as logically following the necessity of rejecting any potency in God. As pure act, God is without composition of any sort.[84] Obviously the doctrine of absolute simplicity poses some difficulties for Trinitarian thought, although Aquinas does not proceed immediately to that doctrine, waiting twenty-four more questions until doing so, prompting suspicion from his detractors that the Trinity is neglected and swamped by unity. However, while the *Summa Theologiae* is often read as a reference book, one where each question stands independent of the others, the text has a pedagogical progression, marshalling question after question in the manner most fit for allowing those insights required for understanding. It should not surprise us, then, that the questions most linked to God's

83. Ibid., 54–61. See also Snell, *Through a Glass Darkly*, 24–29, 71–76.

84. Thomas Aquinas, *Summa Theologica*, I 3.7. Hereafter *ST*.

unity and simplicity (I 3–13) do not digress erratically in discussing God's intellect and will (I 14–26) prior to picking up the Trinity (I 27).

For Thomas, discussion of the Trinity is a question of *procession* in God, a category including both the generation of the Son as well as what the Nicene Creed would label the procession of the Spirit, although he is clear to distinguish an intelligible procession from a physical or natural mode, the relevant distinction is that in intelligible procession the action remains "within the agent."[85] An outward procession, say a change of place or movement of causation, "is necessarily distinct from the source whence it proceeds, whereas, whatever proceeds within by an intelligible procession is not necessarily distinct; indeed, the more perfectly it proceeds, the more closely it is one with the source whence it proceeds."[86] He provides two examples of such intelligible processions, namely, the acts of intellect and will, the very topics discussed extensively in the previous thirteen questions—he prepared the reader well to follow his argument.

In those earlier questions, Aquinas argued that all creaturely perfections exist in God in a superior way, perfectly, without implication of potency, and thus without threatening divine simplicity.[87] God thus has intellect and will in an eminent way, although the mode of the powers differs from how humans possess them, largely in that the powers cannot occasion any movement from potency to act in God.[88] As a result, the act which is God's knowledge cannot differ from the act which is God's being, nor can God's self-knowledge differ from the act of intellect by which God is known: " . . . in God, intellect, and the object understood, and the intelligible species, and His act of understanding are entirely one and the same. Hence when God is said to be understanding, no kind of multiplicity is attached to His substance."[89] Given the lack of composition in God's knowing, understanding "is not an operation proceeding out of the operator, but remaining in him."[90]

85. *ST* I 27.1.

86. *ST* I 27.1, ad 2.

87. *ST* I 14.1, ad 1; I 4.2.

88. Drilling, "Psychological Analogy," 329.

89. *ST* I 14.4.

90. *ST* I 14.4, ad 1.

So, too, the will, which necessarily "follows upon intellect" since will is nothing more than rational appetite for the apprehended good.[91] God both knows and wills substantially, without violation of simplicity; God is the end of all things, utter perfection, knows himself perfectly, and wills the apprehended good, which is to will the divine self. God is love because he wills himself, and the act of willing is not distinct from himself: "The divine will is God's own existence essentially, yet they differ in aspect according to the different ways of understanding them and expressing them . . . ."[92] In God, then, knowing and loving the divine self are not distinct from the divine self.

Having articulated the relation of intellect and will to divine simplicity, Aquinas uses these two acts as the basis from which to grasp the divine processions, claiming that the best analogies are discernible in the intellect where the act remains "within the agent."[93] Like Augustine, he reminds the reader to avoid analogizing from bodies, either in motion or cause, which require an external procession unlike those internal processions of the intellect, whether of knowing or willing.

With respect to the intellect, the divine procession is best understood in its similitude to *intelligible emanation*, the famed inner word or *verbum*, distinct from the outer word or external linguistic utterance.[94] When a concept is formed it can be differentiated from the intellect forming the concept and yet it remains internal to the intellect, it emanates from the power and while distinguished from the power itself it *is* the intellect which forms and understands and possesses the concept. It matters significantly that Aquinas holds to the Aristotelian identity theory of knowing whereby the intellect *becomes* the thing known through being in-formed by the form of the object. In human knowing, unlike God's, extra-mental reality is intelligible by virtue of the thing's form, and when that thing is understood the intellect possesses that very same form in understanding, but the thing is understood properly if and only if the form understood is identical to the intelligibility of the thing. Often this position is treated in a quite mechanical mode, as if the intellect is a cognitive machine somehow extracting form from matter through sensation and subsequently rendering it as knowledge through

---

91. *ST* I 19.1; I 20.1, ad 1.

92. *ST* I 19.2, ad 1.

93. *ST* I 27.1.

94. Ibid; cf. Kilby, "Aquinas," 419.

the magic of abstraction. However unsophisticated the presentation of Thomistic thought, he clearly thinks that the form of the extra-mental reality *is* the form understood; it is the very same form, existing in either extra-mental *or* intentional reality. Of course, since God knows the divine self perfectly, his being, intellect, and verbum involve no potency, so knowing is an identity for God, albeit in a way more perfect than human knowing. The verbum, the inner word, is an intelligible emanation, a procession, and is differentiated from the intellect without thereby being external to the intellect, just as the Verbum, the divine Word, proceeds from the Father, and is not the Father, but is of one being with the Father:

> The act of human understanding in ourselves is not the substance itself of the intellect; hence the word which proceeds within us by intelligible operation is not of the same nature as the source whence it proceeds; so the idea of generation cannot be properly and fully applied to it. But the divine act of intelligence is the very substance itself of the one who understands. The Word proceeding therefore proceeds as subsisting in the same nature; and so is properly called begotten, and Son.[95]

Recalling the broad category of procession which here includes both the generation of the Word and the procession of the Spirit, Aquinas has explained generation in terms of the intelligible emanation of the verbum, and does something similar with the procession of the Spirit, although utilizing the analogue of will to do so. Just as the word was divine self-knowledge and its internal procession, so also "love expresses divine self-love" in a way illustrating "how distinction of the three in God can really exist even within God's radical unity."[96] His explanation of this is rather succinct; having introduced the argument's apparatus for the intelligible emanation of the verbum he utilizes it quite briefly for the will, claiming a broad similarity between the two:

> The procession of the Word is by way of an intelligible operation. The operation of the will within ourselves involves also another procession, that of love, whereby the object loved is in the lover; as, by the conception of the word, the object spoken of or understood is in the intelligent agent. Hence, besides the procession of

95. *ST* I 27.2, ad 2; cf. Ormerod, "Psychological Analogy," 283; Drilling, "Psychological Analogy," 330.

96. Drilling, "Psychological Analogy," 330–31.

the Word in God, there exists in Him another procession called
the procession of love.[97]

The procession of love is such that the object loved remains *in* the
lover, as an internal procession just as with intellect, although differences exist. First, for Aquinas there is a certain order in the relation of
intellect to will, for nothing can be loved until apprehended as a good
in the intellect, and, second, whereas the intellect is "made actual by the
object understood . . . the will is made actual . . . by its having a certain
inclination to the thing willed."[98] The intellect is actualized by its identity
with the thing known, but the will is actualized by "way of impulse and
movement towards an object," although in God the object known and
loved is the divine self towards which God does not need to move to
attain.[99]

The Analogy, Love, and the Pivot

All this articulates the brief basics of Aquinas' articulation of the psychological analogy, and it demonstrates some necessary relationship
between intellect and love in that love requires intellect, but it has not
demonstrated either that love is necessary for knowledge or that Aquinas
has attained this knowledge through a reflexive pivot (noetic exegesis)
upon his own operations, although we argue for both points below.

It is true that the pedagogical ordering of the text provides a lengthy
discussion of intellect and will preceding the two processions in the
analogy, but at best this shows that Aquinas has defined the terms prior
to their use, not that he has grounded the definitions in reflexivity. We
should not expect too much from him on this matter, for he is not writing in a critical mode after the turn to the subject in modernity, and he is
clearly availing himself of Aristotelian theory much more evidently than
Augustinian interiority. The mere fact that he supports the psychological
analogy is not itself evidence of interiority as a method, or at least not
as we are supposing it here. So we can expect the interiority to be somewhat muted, for even if the psychology of Aristotle and Aquinas "has too
uncanny an accuracy to be possible without the greatest introspective
skill . . . it remains that they did not thematize their use, did not elevate

97. *ST* I 27.3.
98. *ST* I 27.4.
99. Ibid.

it to a reflexively elaborated technique."[100] Note, however, the admission that Aquinas did not explicitly elaborate a method of reflexivity does not imply that he did not perform reflexively or that there is no evidence to this effect, just that he did not explicitly formulate his method.

What is this inner word? Lonergan claims that Aquinas means by *verbum* "the immanent object of intellectual operation," which requires determining what is meant by (1) immanent object and (2) intellectual operation.[101] Aquinas hints at a similar definition when stating that "by the very fact of understanding there proceeds something within us, which is a conception of the object understood, a conception issuing from our intellectual power and proceeding from our knowledge of that object."[102] Now, Aquinas links the inner word to understanding, for it is by the "fact of understanding" that the *verbum* issues and proceeds, and the *verbum* is the conception of the "object understood." Immanent object, then, would be what issues or proceeds from understanding, and the intellectual operation would seem to be understanding itself. Understanding seems to be, thus, not only a state or condition attained, "knowledge of that object," but also the operation or act by which knowledge is reached. So to grasp what is meant by Lonergan's definition and its elements of (1) immanent object and (2) intellectual operation requires a grasp of understanding, which is the operation by which the immanent object proceeds, or emanates.

The inner word is not the outer word of speech or imagination but rather the concept which grounds and sources the outer word. As concept, it supplies the object of thought and is the means through which the intellect knows things, recalling the identity theory of knowledge whereby the intellect becomes the thing known insofar as the inner word *is* the thing known in an intentional mode.[103] Further, the inner word is not simply present or innate but emerges at the end of thought, once something is understood, but not before, and while it is distinct from the power of understanding itself, the inner word would seem to emerge simultaneously with actually understanding something.[104] As

100. Lonergan, *Verbum*, 5–6.

101. Ibid., 10.

102. *ST* I 27.1.

103. Lonergan, *Verbum*, 14–21.

104. Ibid., 22–23.

Aquinas puts it, quoting Augustine, for us "word 'cannot exist without actual thought,' . . . by actual thought we form an internal word."[105]

There is an inadequate version of the concept which overlooks the actual thinking, the operations and process of understanding by which we understand, and assumes that the concept "was not the result of a conscious act—*emanatio intelligibilis*—but was . . . produced unconsciously by the metaphysical machinery of that great 'black box,' the human mind."[106] This *conceptualism* neglects understanding, the operations of actual thinking, and in its commitment to an unconscious production cannot consistently engage in noetic exegesis—one cannot pivot reflexively and experience an unconscious production. However, Aquinas' more adequate *intellectualism* provides for that possibility, for if the operations of actual thinking are the means by which the verbum emerges, and if those operations are performed in *actual, conscious thinking*, then one can advert consciousness towards consciousness, thereby rendering as an object of thought the process by which thought produces objects of thought—one can attain a verbum about verbum, as awkward as that sounds.

This notion is entirely consistent with the Thomistic approach to knowledge which insists, along with Aristotle, that there is no immediate means to grasp the nature of a thing in intellectual intuition; rather, natures are differentiated by potencies, potencies are identified by their acts, and acts are distinguished by their objects.[107] Self-knowledge is no different, for there is no immediate grasp of the essence of the self, but rather that essence is known by grasping potencies, known by acts, known by objects—start with the objects to understand the nature, start with what is understood. Note the reflexivity made possible by this account: we have no direct grasp of our essence but would know ourselves by grasping the object of knowledge, but the object of knowledge *is* the inner word through which extra-mental objects are understood. If understanding were thoroughly understood, one would know both one's own self and the operations by which everything is understood.

The preceding is still an outline of the position and we will not here provide a detailed exegesis of Lonergan's reading. That is the subject of Chapter 3 and would result in a good deal of redundancy; for the mo-

---

105. *ST* I 93.7.

106. Byrne, "Fabric of Lonergan's Thought," 46.

107. Lonergan, *Verbum*, 4.

ment the task is merely to show the reflexivity built into the psychological analogy. But to articulate the role of love a few brief elements must
be described, all of which receive more detailed and nuanced discussion
in the further chapters.

work

The inner word is not produced automatically or unconsciously,
which is why understanding the world and ourselves takes work, inquiry. Humans are in potency relative to knowledge, we do not begin by
knowing but come to know through a process of reasoning, and we do
not know until that thinking is completed:

> Conceptualization comes as the term and product of a process of
> reasoning. As long as the reasoning, the fluctuation of discourse
> continues, the inner word is as yet unuttered. But it is also true
> that as long as the reasoning continues, we do not as yet under-
> stand; for until the inner word is uttered, we are not understand-
> ing but only thinking in order to understand.[108]

What is reasoning, the activity, the "actual thinking"? For Thomas,
it is the process of *abstraction*, a notion which conceptualism tends
to think of as a unconscious process of extraction of form, but which
Thomas' intellectualism considers to be a conscious, psychological fact
which can be noticed and studied in its own right. Abstraction takes a
variety of forms including abstracting from that which is irrelevant to
explanation, such as that a scientific experiment took place in Stockholm
as opposed to Chicago, also abstracting from those sense data irrelevant
to cause, such as the size or color of a triangle in a geometry problem,
and also abstracting from matter entirely to conceive of metaphysical
theorems of being per se.[109] But in a more concrete sense, abstraction
occurs by the power of the agent intellect discerning intelligibility in
sense data (phantasm). This is a point that Aquinas makes concretely
by appeal to noetic experience, a kind of reflexivity: " . . . anyone can
experience this of himself, that when he tries to understand something,
he forms certain phantasms to serve him by way of examples. . . . "[110]
Still, sense data is not itself intelligible and cannot be the cause of knowing, for sense data "require to be made actually intelligible by the active

108. Ibid., 51.
109. Ibid, 54–55.
110. *ST* I 84.7.

intellect," an "intellectual operation" by which there is insight into the phantasm.[111]

Now this operation of active intellect is accessible to all, for it is the immanent light by which we render the world intelligible to ourselves, and scrutiny of the active intellect is the means by which we understand understanding. What is striking is how mundane and common this is—we engage the active intellect by which we abstract and reason and eventually understand/produce the inner word whenever we inquire and wish to know. That is, whenever we question. Questions can be engaged in reflexively, we need only to ask about the nature and function of questions, and, as we see in Chapter 3, there are a few basic questions governing our knowing and doing: What is it? Is it? Is it to be done? And these questions are the point of education as well as the norms of and means to authenticity and conversion.

Questions, however, arise only when one desires to know, when one cares, when one values the knowing or doing, and they do not arise nearly as often in the dull, improperly in the wicked, but frequently in the engaged, systematically in the wise, and responsibly in the virtuous. In other words, the psychological analogy, worked through a bit, even if in a brief and truncated form here, reveals not only that love follows the knowledge or apprehension of the good, but love also precedes apprehension, for without care there are no questions, and without questions and inquiry there is no understanding. Further, all this can be demonstrated reflexively—just ask, does understanding happen for you when you do not question, or do insights tend to arise and accumulate and correct and develop insofar as you want to know? How many times just in this chapter did you care enough to ask, or challenge, or re-read, and were those questions the conditions of your insights and judgments about the chapter? If we care enough to ask, we will care enough to know, and care is a love of the real, a wondering stance towards what is.

CONCLUSION

The preceding is creative retrieval, a productive reading of texts admitting to reading backwards, as it were, asking questions about texts and thinkers they may not themselves have asked, but still claiming textual evidence for the reading. We are under no illusions that these three

---

111. *ST* I 84.6.

thinkers would articulate themselves as we have articulated them, nor would we claim to have concocted the readings out of whole cloth. Texts occupy a space within the development of thought, often encouraging and prompting the development, so it should not surprise us that we can read texts with the questions of Heidegger or Lonergan in mind and find profit in the task.

The tradition was not a monolithic commitment to the "thinking things" model of anthropology but on occasion gave privilege to love as the primary condition for what it meant to be human, and certainly for what it meant for humans to know. Further, the tradition was sophisticated enough to allow basic, if non-explicit, attempts at noetic exegesis—although that methodology must wait hundreds of years to become thematized; even then, thinkers concerned with the thematization of noetic exegesis, figures like Voegelin, Lonergan, Heidegger, and Charles Taylor, turned to the philosophers discussed in this chapter for guidance. We turn now to these more contemporary explorations of love.

2

Martin Heidegger, Charles Taylor, and the Caring Person

Our retrieval of an anthropology of love continues by tracing Heidegger's early turn to Augustine and subsequent hermeneutics of facticity. Charles Taylor is also helpful, providing an account of engaged subjectivity and the moral space making up personal identity. For both, there is no person without a horizon, and there is no horizon without love, so love determines the person, and authenticity moves into central focus.

In the previous chapter we indicated that the turn to subjectivity is somewhat out of favor, especially in its linking to Trinitarian thought in the psychological analogy; with the concept of authenticity we encounter another notion viewed with some suspicion. Deeply entrenched in contemporary consciousness, authenticity's genealogy is complicated and disputed, although certainly Heidegger contributed to authenticity's currency in the last century, mediating the notion to existentialism and general culture.[1] Authenticity has its opponents, however. Not only postmodernists suspicious of any presentation of harmonious, unitary subjectivity, but also those with ethical systems rooted in static accounts of human nature or metaphysical biology, as well as a great many thinkers, more than a few influenced by Tocqueville, identifying in authenticity a pathway to personal and political trivialization, self-indulgence, and endless narcissism.[2] On the Continent, perhaps the strongest criticism came from Theodor Adorno, who identified in the cult of authenticity

1. Braman, *Meaning and Authenticity*, 3–7.

2. For example, Robert Bellah, Phillipe Beneton, Allan Bloom, Mary Ann Glendon, Christopher Lasch, Peter Augustine Lawler, Alasdair MacIntyre, and Jonathan Sacks.

a secularized and corrupted religion, shorn of transcendence, in which it mattered not what was professed so long as it was professed, a great trivialization as well as a moral calamity, particularly with memory of the *Shoah* and Heidegger's "authentic" involvement with the Nazis in the immediate background.[3]

While we go beyond Heidegger and Taylor to the thought of Bernard Lonergan in subsequent chapters, the two are important for any retrieval of intentionality for anthropology. While Heidegger's account of authenticity has serious lacunae, his pivoting to care as a primary category of human existence provides a helpful correction to the disengaged rationalism of so much modern philosophy, and, moreover, places intentionality firmly *alongside* relation to others, sociality, language, embodiment, heritage, place, and temporality rather than remaining trapped within an account of subjectivity privileging a merely mental and punctual self. Taylor, too, articulates an account of the person always already beyond themselves, with others, and for whom genuine authenticity requires a form of self-transcendence escaping those degraded forms of authenticity haunting contemporary thought and life.

HEIDEGGER AND THE HERMENEUTICS OF FACTICITY

In his 1921 lectures on Augustine's *Confessions*, Heidegger ruminates on the Augustinian insight that humans are a question to themselves.[4] Standing before a God who knows all things, Augustine wonders what it might mean to confess to one from whom nothing is concealed, and he "wants to dare confess himself . . . only what he knows about himself," and yet he does not know everything about himself but "wants to confess that too."[5] He has become a question to himself.

Knowing that he loves God, he does not know what he loves in loving God, for God is not known: "Augustine attempts to find an answer . . . by investigating what there is which is worthy of love, and by asking whether there is something among them which God himself is . . . what suffices . . . or saturates, that which, in the love of God, he intends."[6] Already distancing himself from the modern problematic and its de-

3. Braman, *Meaning and Authenticity*, 5–7.

4. Heidegger, "Augustine and Neo-Platonism." See also Lawrence, "Hermeneutic Revolution and the Future of Theology," and "Lonergan's Hermeneutics of Facticity."

5. Heidegger, "Augustine and Neo-Platonism," 129–30.

6. Ibid.

mand for objective distance, Heidegger claims that Augustine cannot confess himself with an "attitude . . . of natural-scientific research," but must turn inward to his own soul and to the *memoria* in which he meets and recalls himself.[7] To put it another way, to find the answer of himself, he turns to love, for "what determines the answers we discover to the question that we are for ourselves is . . . only disclosed by our loving. What we love massively conditions our concrete solution to the problem of living together."[8] Consequently, Heidegger finds in his retrieval of Augustine an ally in overcoming the "ahistorical, atemporal, decontextualizing of the self" endemic to modern philosophy, and a path forward to the breakthroughs of *Being and Time*.[9] Heidegger stresses that search for the truth was "contorted through Greek philosophy" with its concerns for correspondence and the metaphysics of substances, but that Augustine allows for the search to "be taken back into the existential-historical unity" of historical-factical lived existence.[10] Everyone prefers truth to falsehood as naturally as they want the happy life, Heidegger says, linking the two, for "a happy life is the joy of truth, and truth is experienced as joy when encountered in one's lived experience. So all are "somehow rejoicing in, and making an effort towards, the truth" of existence, for in "factical life, human beings somehow intimate something right, love in it and for it as something significant," and yet "why are they nonetheless not in the *beata vita* . . . why does the joy which corresponds to such *veritas* not live in them?"[11] Humans, it would seem, "do wish that the 'truth' reveals itself to them . . . but they themselves close themselves off against it. . . . "[12]

The care of Augustine is transposed into the *curare*, or "being concerned" of phenomenology, and *curare*, for Heidegger, is the basic constitutive character of factical life, concrete selfhood, including our troubles and temptations.[13] If one was concerned for God alone, if one was continent, one would not be scattered in many directions, and yet

7. Ibid., 130, 131, 137.

8. Lawrence, "Lonergan's Hermeneutics of Facticity," 427.

9. Heidegger, *Being and Time*.

10. Heidegger, "Augustine and Neo-Platonism," 146.

11. Ibid., 146–47.

12. Ibid., 148.

13. Ibid., 151.

one is scattered "into the manifold and . . . absorbed in the dispersion."[14]
Life is full of troubles (*molestia*) to occupy concern, and moves within
a temporal oscillation between grief and joy, prosperity and adversity.[15]
Human life is "nothing but constant temptation," and "Augustine experiences factical life" in the "fundamental character" of *tentatio*, and so is
"necessarily a burden to himself."[16] In *tentatio* humans finds themselves
and cannot know themselves other than through the *tentatio* of concrete
and performative human living, and in a lifetime of burdens, judged
over and against the relation to God, both human existence and God
come to be known.

Heidegger did not work out clearly the relationship of sin and *molestia*, despite his dependence on Augustine. He would appear to identify factical, historical existence (*Faktizität*) with *molestia*, which would
render sinfulness part of human nature, or reduce sinfulness to mere
finitude. Another way of posing this would be to ask whether fallenness
meant a fall from grace or simply human finitude, and Heidegger seems
to reduce it to finitude, to temporality and its oscillations, at least in part
influenced by his secularizing of Augustine with his use of Aristotle in
developing the hermeneutics of facticity of *Being and Time*.[17] Leaving
sin and grace aside, Heidegger interprets the troubles and temptations of
Augustine as "simply challenges to human seriousness and authenticity,"
as the idle-chatter and trivial lack of self-appropriation of the inauthentic self.[18]

Dasein Is Care

The pattern of care and fallenness is repeated in *Being and Time*, where
Heidegger wishes to overcome the easy forgetfulness of the question of
Being and its meaning. Inquiry into Being is made difficult in that every
inquiry "gets guided beforehand by what is sought," and so we must be
vaguely familiar enough with Being to know what we are looking for; we
have already an average everyday understanding of being.[19] Our inter-

---

14. Ibid., 152.

15. Lawrence, "Hermeneutic Revolution," 333–34.

16. Ibid.

17. Ibid., 335.

18. Ibid.

19. Heidegger, *Being and Time*, 25.

rogation could be about entities or substances in the world, but which ones would be the best place to start when Being is universal, related to all that is? Heidegger suggests that the interrogation should be of those entities who interrogate, of those entities for whom the question of the meaning of being matters:

> Thus to work out the question of Being adequately, we must make an entity—the inquirer—transparent in his own Being. This very asking of the question is an entity's mode of *Being*; and as such it gets its essential character from what is inquired about—namely, Being. This entity which each of us is himself and which includes inquiring as one of the possibilities of its Being, we shall denote by the term *Dasein*.[20]

Dasein, the interrogator, also serves as that which is interrogated, with inquiry itself a hint to the mode of Being of Dasein. Knowing is "fueled by desire, it is not neutral" and so there is a fundamental reflexivity (even circularity) to the inquiry, for the study of being will be the study of the one caring about the question.[21]

Methodologically, *Being and Time* is placed firmly in the turn to the subject, a move which Heidegger later rejected, bemoaning its continued linkage to "phenomenology as propped on egology," and still dependent on consciousness, *Bewußtsein*, in a Kantian or Cartesian sense.[22] His purpose in the text, however, is not a departure from the general question of Being, but a judgment that the question is best understood by a grasp of our own concern for the question. First grasping the Being of Dasein, he intends to circle back in moves of retrieval and reinterpretation to the broad question, but the "ontological analytic of Dasein in general is what makes up fundamental ontology, so that Dasein functions as that entity which in principle is to be *interrogated* beforehand as to its Being . . . that entity which already comports itself, in its Being, towards what we are asking about. . . . "[23]

Access to Dasein begins not from some abstract (thus alienated) theoretical conception of the human essence, but in the concrete situatedness of everyday living, the way Dasein (being-there) exists always

---

20. Ibid., 27.

21. Marsh, "Self-Appropriation," 57; cf. Heidegger, *Being and Time*, 27.

22. Lawrence, "Hermeneutic Revolution," 338; cf. Lawrence, "Fragility of Consciousness," 55–94; Lawrence, "Lonergan, the Integral Postmodern?," 95–122.

23. Heidegger, *Being and Time*, 35.

already in the world—Dasein does not exist in the "in here" of mental space, but *there*, in the projects and tools and relations of the world, and certainly the Cartesian problem of getting back out-there is for Heidegger the sort of issue emerging long after ordinary Dasein has abstracted themselves from their concrete existence. Consequently, in interrogating Dasein's mode of Being, Heidegger dwells on an exploration of average everydayness in which Dasein's fundamental mode of being-there is to be-with others (*Mitsein*). Consequently, the study of Being begins with catching "ourselves in the act of everyday existence" in which we are not distinterested observers of human nature, "but *engaged actors*," relating to our Being not "primarily through knowledge of self-consciousness, but through acting, through capably dealing with the beings around us."[24]

Dasein is engaged with the world because the world matters to Dasein, as does the question of Being. In fact, the very Being of Dasein is that things *matter*, or as Heidegger puts it, "Dasein's Being is care (*Sorge*)."[25] It has concern for Being, its own as well as the world's, and for Dasein the world is articulated and ordered around what matters, what is pressing, what concerns Dasein. Care is the transcendental condition of possibility of being-there for Dasein, for the world is disclosed and opened because of Dasein's standing towards it in engagement, the responsibilities and projects and possibilities envisioned and enacted by Dasein.

Care has a fundamental structure and is comprised of "facticity (thrownness), existence (projection), and falling."[26] As thrown, Dasein "has been brought into its 'there', but *not* of its own accord . . . it never comes back behind its thrownness is such a way that it might first release this 'that-it-is-and-has-to-be from *its Being*-its-Self."[27] We find ourselves already existing in a world, as factical, and Heidegger emphasizes the role of mood, or attunement, in disclosing the fact of our being in the world; attunement also reveals our past history, for we find ourselves already thrown, having already been here, "always disclosed as that entity . . . delivered over in its Being."[28] Moodedness is fundamental and

---

24. Polt, *Heidegger*, 45.
25. Heidegger, *Being and Time*, 329.
26. Ibid.
27. Ibid., 329–30.
28. Ibid., 173.

cannot be excised, and we are always attuned to the world in a certain way, with the mood disclosing the world in some particular, thus partial, form. Consequently, any goal of a perfectly objective, perfectly universal vantage point is naive, for as thrown we always, and can only, have a world disclosed in a certain way, under a certain guise, from a particular stance, from a certain engagement.[29]

Not only the world, but Dasein is revealed by mood, for "whether explicitly or not, it finds itself in its thrownness. In a state-of-mind Dasein is always brought before itself, and has always found itself, not in the sense of coming across itself by perceiving itself, but in the sense of finding itself in the mood that it has."[30] This self-disclosure occurs "*prior to* all cognition and volition," and so is a more primordial form of self-disclosure than the *cogito* ever could be, for only once disclosed to itself as existing could the Cartesian *cogito* have the capacity to interrogate itself, or care to.

If thrownness, or facticity, is the first structure of care revealing the already-ness of being-there, a past, *existence* as a second structure of care discloses Dasein's future projects. Finding ourselves in a world, in a certain mood, entities are disclosed to us in a variety of different modes, and we understand and interpret these entities and our relation to them. Understanding (*Verstehen*) is a stand, or way of letting things be involved with our care in this or that way, in this or that stance, so as to disclose things in relation to various possibilities of our projects. For the sake of being an athlete we disclose the being of a ball; for the sake of being a good parent to a toddler we disclose a different being for the same ball.[31] Having taken a stance towards the ball, I can form an assertion about the ball in a propositional form, although usually there is no reason to do so, and my interpretation comes not necessarily in my words or concepts but in the projects and uses with which I approach the ball. Understanding, therefore, is a way of projecting possibilities, of possible interpretations.

Every interpretation occurs within the past which is already given, including Dasein's own thrownness, but Dasein is not static and their Being is not merely what they have been or now are, for Dasein is also what they can be; Dasein, thus, can interpret themselves in light of their

29. Polt, *Heidegger*, 67.

30. Heidegger, *Being and Time*, 174.

31. Polt, *Heidegger*, 68.

future projects, and the entities and the world are interpreted in light of these forward projections. Of course, possibilities are conditioned by the significance Dasein already has for itself and its world; having already interpreted entities *as* this or *as* that, possibilities bring along previous interpretations, for Dasein approaches possibilities from what has already been: "Whenever something is interpreted as something, the interpretation will be founded essentially upon fore-having, fore-sight, and fore-conception. An interpretation is never a presuppositionless apprehending of something presented to us."[32]

Under the guise of some interpretation, entities are revealed *as* a this or that, and as disclosed the entity has meaning, although meaning arises from our ability to project possibility—things mean because they matter to some way in which I engage them, otherwise they would not mean. As such, entities mean because they refer to Dasein's projects, inhabiting a location within the totality of the projects, for Dasein's world is a totality of references, which is to say a totality of projects or engagements. No entity stands alone in some isolated atomic understanding of perception or significance, but all are linked together in a series of articulations, with this connected to that and that to this other in the web of purposes, uses, interpretations. The articulation of the world into intelligibility is what Heidegger calls discourse, the condition of possibility of language.[33]

The third structure of care, fallenness, borrowed but secularized from Augustine, deserves longer treatment.

Fallenness: The Cares of das Man

We are not engaged actors in isolation, and in our average everydayness we exist with others in a common world of meanings and interpretations. Unlike the Cartesian *cogito* struggling to convince itself that others exist, we are not normally reflexive and self-consciously aware of ourselves as distinct, solitary individuals; we tend to exist alongside others in pretty much the same way that everyone else exists: "I do *not* normally exist as myself—I exist as just anyone, as no one in particular."[34] So while Dasein "is in each case one's *own* . . . for the most part, one does

32. Heidegger, *Being and Time*, 190–91.
33. Ibid., 203.
34. Polt, *Heidegger*, 60.

not distinguish oneself."[35] Consequently, we simply do not gain access to ourselves through the form of introspection which thinks of itself as a solitary inner-gazing of the mind but rather are inescapably social and encultured beings.

Usually, one does not own one's own existence as one's own, but lives as "the they" do, as *das Man* does. When one is inauthentic, one is the they-self, for then "they" determine one's own possibilities and projects "within the limits which have been established with the 'they's' averageness."[36] Authenticity, however, living as one's own self, is not a fundamental departure from the "they" but rather a mode of being alongside and with others: "Authenticity does not involve jettisoning one's own tradition—which is impossible—but *clear-sightedly* and *resolutely* pursuing a possibility that is opened up by this tradition."[37] Consequently, it is not as if living along with the "they" is a moral failing, it is not, because the "they" is an inescapable element of our ontology, "*it belongs to Dasein's positive constitution.*"[38]

Still, our status as embroiled with the "they" makes self-interpretation difficult, not only because the relations of average everydayness are usually not thematized, but also because "covered over and distorted" by the patterns of *das Man*, particularly the "they's" penchant for idle-chatter, gossip, curiosity, and various forms of dissipation into the "mundane aspects of human living with little or no reflection."[39] In giving our own selves over to the inauthentic they-self, we are distracted from our ownmost selves by the cares and concerns borrowed from the "they"— *molestia* and *tentatio* secularized.

The need to resolutely determine one's own possibilities becomes hidden, and everything becomes "concernful absorption in the world we encounter as closest to us . . . and the 'they' Articulates the referential context of significance."[40] Meaning is held in common, automatic, unchosen, and the "they" maintains, even enforces, the averageness "which it regards as valid . . . which it grants success . . . it keeps watch over everything exceptional that thrusts itself to the fore" in a leveling down

35. Heidegger, *Being and Time*, 154.

36. Ibid., 164, 167.

37. Polt, *Heidegger*, 63.

38. Heidegger, *Being and Time*, 167.

39. Braman, *Meaning and Authenticity*, 10.

40. Heidegger, *Being and Time*, 165.

into "publicness . . . control[ling] every way in which the world and Dasein get interpreted."[41] In publicness every possibility "gets passed off as something familiar and accessible to everyone" and Dasein is relieved of the burden of its own existence and the determination of its ownmost possibilities.[42]

Of course, it is only in this space that Dasein encounters anything in the world, including its own self, and so the "they" and they-self make possible the disclosure of the world of significance, of meaningful referentiality and value, and without *das Man* there would be no Dasein—Dasein exists as being-with. The very possibility of things disclosing themselves to us, revealing their truth, depends on the disclosure of sociality, and we live in truth as a result. But we live simultaneously in untruth, because fallenness results in superficial interpretations of everything, a closing off of possibilities and a hiding of what could be grasped. Things are revealed, but in a closed off manner. Only the temporal closing of one's own death allows authenticity, for only in the recognition of Being-towards-death (*Sein zum Tode*) does one's ownmost possibility emerge, and with it the possibility of resoluteness in other projects and concerns which all end in death. Being-towards-death reveals the truth of things, their "ripeness" and "end," a revelation linked closely to mood.[43]

Mood, especially that of anxiety, is a somewhat rare rupture of the familiar and usual chains of significance; the distractions of everydayness are thrown back to disclose Dasein's ownmost possibility, which is nothingness. Fallenness generally covers over this possibility in the routine of borrowed meanings and projects, but this tranquility is inauthentic, it is "a constant temptation . . . Being-in-the-world is in itself tempting,"[44] in a mode similar to the *tentatio* of Augustine.[45] *Tentatio* "drives one into uninhibited hustle," into the various inauthentic concerns (*molestia*) of the fallen, an "alienation [which] closes off from Dasein its authenticity and possibility." In anxiety, however, Dasein is revealed as one for whom Being matters, and in this care can choose identity, although not in a completely undefined way, for the past has

41. Ibid.
42. Ibid.
43. Heidegger, *Being and Time*, 274–90.
44. Ibid., 221.
45. Ibid., 222.

shaped what is, and Dasein cannot leap out of the past. Since Dasein is care, Dasein is *never* separated from the world, from others, from projects or purposes; since Being matters to Dasein, it is always already, and always ahead-of-time engaged with meaning. We are worlded, there is for us reality, only because our very being is care. Our loves run ahead of us to what we *could be*, and what the world could be, because our loves have already made us what we *have been* and what we *now are*. Love makes the world what it is.

CHARLES TAYLOR AND ENGAGED AGENCY

Heidegger's notion of authenticity is grounded in the notion of appropriating embeddedness or involvement; humans simply do not exist as disengaged or uninvolved with their world, they do not stand outside a world distinctly "out there" as opposed to the "in here" of our subjective inner life. Instead, we are always already involved and engaged with the world in our projects and concerns and cares, something that Heidegger, Plato, Augustine, and Aquinas all articulate in their own way, and with varying levels of sophistication.

Charles Taylor carries forward the project of "engaged human agency," in some opposition to reductive naturalism.[46] Influenced by the phenomenology of Maurice Merleau-Ponty, Taylor thinks we are "condemned to meaning," with lives "structured by inescapable layers of meaning or significance."[47] This is primarily true because things are not-indifferent to us, they matter, and we are always engaged with the world because we are in it; there is no dispassionate or disengaged rationality viewing the world as a camera might.[48] In the brief sections to follow, we articulate the core of Taylor's anthropology of engaged agency, as well as something of his account of authenticity which follows from the anthropology.

Condemned to Involvement

Taylor claims that authenticity is a contemporary moral ideal often "degraded but . . . worthwhile in itself," although retrieval is needed to

---

46. Taylor, "Engaged Agency and Background in Heidegger."
47. Smith, *Charles Taylor*, 1.
48. Ibid., 7.

recover its normative and valuable contribution.[49] Whereas the ideal of authenticity is "being true to oneself," it easily becomes, in reality as well as caricature, an ethic of trivial self-indulgence, relativism, and even absurdity as those striving to be themselves become conformists in their dependence on ready-made and fashionable identities.[50] Many opponents of authenticity view it as an abandonment of standards and criteria, either those rooted in human nature or philosophical methodology, and suspect that a soft relativism of individualism inevitably follows, with each person claiming a right to determine their own sense of what really matters in a "centring on the self and a concomitant sitting out, or even unawareness, of the greater issues or concerns that transcend the self, be they religious, political, historical."[51]

Taylor counters such objections with both a sophisticated history of selfhood and a moral ontology, with a unifying theme the role of meaning for selfhood. For Taylor, we are condemned to meaning. Even perception is laden with meaning, for like animals we tend to note what interests us while disregarding what does not, like how a predator perceives the mouse somewhat differently than it does a rock—those things which have significance tend to stand out in perception.[52] Further, consciousness would always seem to be intentional, "of" or "about" something, but Taylor learns from Merleau-Ponty that the directedness of consciousness is compounded by "intentionality-as-significance," for intentionality is not just "about" but always directed-for or towards something.[53] On a naïve model of perception, our experience of the world would be relatively undifferentiated, just one sensation after another pulsing into consciousness as discrete atomic experiences. But experience is not really like this, for the perception is already significant, not only because of what we are interested in noting but also because phenomenal objects bear witness to structures of significance, revealing or covering over other objects and purposes in a nexus of significance. Imagine the difficulty of perceiving a tool, a hammer, without situating it within a context of its purposes, of nails and picture frames, of use and behavior.

49. Taylor, *Ethics of Authenticity*, 23.
50. Ibid.
51. Ibid., 14.
52. Ibid., 2.
53. Ibid., 27.

We tend to relate desire to purpose and action, but we interpret rather than perceive the meaning of an action, often when the significance of the action is unclear or complicated, and interpretations are not always without ambiguity or conflict. At times interpreting an action reveals to us a saturation of significance, a weight to the action somewhat more than was expected, and even some desires themselves are interpreted by us as more significant than other desires, more worthwhile to have and pursue. A momentary interest in a dessert seems to us less worthwhile than health, even though both are positioned within the space of how we conceive and value our own worth. We can be disappointed that we chose dessert over health, especially if we promised ourselves to moderate our desires because a loved one asked us to do so; consequently, the interpretations and significance of desires includes an interpretation of our own identity and value, the way of life around which our identity revolves, and in that light some desires and projects seem starkly more worthwhile than others.[54]

Desires operate within a structure of significance and evaluation, with some interpretations serving as terminal, from which we situate ourselves, our desires, and our self-interpretations in relief to those terminal ideals; for us, they are normative and constitutive of how we understand our identity. Despite the importance these highest values play in our lives, identifying and understanding them is frustratingly hard. Our identities develop and change over time, we exist within a variety of communities and their competing identity claims, and we are aware that other identities and values exist, sometimes at odds with our own, and yet seem highly successful and desirable. Our identity-shaping values themselves can lose their obviousness, can become less desirable than we once imagined, and as a result the narrative of our life can alter.

Given the link between intentionality and identity, Taylor rejects the subject-object split of the Cartesian imagination, with subjectivity disengaged from the world behind the veil of ideas and wondering if it will ever be in contact with the world again. Any adequate description of a human being as intentional must include the directedness or purposive nature of intentionality and how the person's consciousness always exhibits a stance, a comportment by which the agent interprets and "copes" with the world, thus revealing their deep engagement with the world and the impossibility of having any identity without engaged

54. Ibid.

subjectivity.[55] To perceive is already to be caught up into "an overall sense of ourselves and our world. . . . "[56] Consequently, since even to perceive is to be caught up into the drama of our own identity and the interpretation of our own self, Taylor claims that human selfhood has an intrinsic and inescapable moral dimension—morality is a necessary dimension of subjectivity.[57]

In an early work, Taylor distinguished strong and weak evaluations, or between two stances that persons take when they evaluate.[58] Borrowing from Harry Frankfurt's distinction of first- and second-order desires, Taylor agrees that humans share with animals behaviors which satisfy first-order desires for food, safety, or reproduction, but unlike animals humans have desires about their own desires, evaluating their own desires and ascribing praise and blame. Taylor asks another question, however, about the ways we go about evaluating our desires, and argues we can do so either according to a strong or weak evaluation. Strong evaluations judge the worth of desires whereas weak evaluations "weigh alternatives" to judge the degree and amount of satisfaction made possible.[59] In other words, weak evaluations deliberate on the instrumentality of actions, and are based in satisfaction, whereas strong evaluations judge the worth of the desires themselves based on relatively stable and important interpretations of one's identity—strong evaluations place preferences in relief against what is most valued to a person, thus revealing how they interpret their own selves.[60]

Since strong evaluations involve claims about the self, Taylor concludes that human subjectivity is irreducibly linked to morality, with morality part of the ontology of human subjectivity—we are *valuing and evaluating beings*.[61] Strong evaluators have a sense of self and its depth quite distinct from weak evaluators, and the ability to understand one's own self as a strong evaluator reveals that selfhood is not a property one possesses the way a substance "has" properties but is understood insofar as one grasps one's own ability to distinguish worth.

55. Baker, *Tayloring Reformed Epistemology*, 107.

56. Ibid.

57. Smith, *Taylor*, 87.

58. Taylor, *Human Agency and Language*, 15–19.

59. Ibid., 23.

60. Smith, *Taylor*, 90.

61. Baker, *Tayloring Reformed Epistemology*, 109.

If there were only weak evaluations, an agent faced with some choice would perhaps understand that a plurality of preferences were at play, possibly pulling in different directions, and yet the agent would have not much more than a sense of feeling some desires more strongly than others. An agent capable of strong evaluation, on the other hand, judges some desires as worth more, as superior in quality. Importantly, the qualitative framework works its way into the desires themselves, as wanting to live a good and worthwhile life is itself desired.[62]

Taylor frames worth in the language of value—*strong values* are those goods serving as standards against which we judge the worth of desires as well as the worth of our choices and identity. In *Sources of the Self* he identifies three categories of strong values, (1) those goods "which cluster around the sense that human life is to be respected . . . ," (2) our sense of "what constitutes a rich, meaningful life," and (3) those notions "concerned with dignity . . . the characteristics by which we think of ourselves as commanding (or failing to command) the respect of those around us."[63] Distinct times and cultures understand and weigh the goods differently, but the distinguishing mark of modernity is its problematic stance towards the second category of goods, namely the sense of a good life. All cultures have questions related to this category, but tend to view the framework which answers these questions as being unproblematic or unquestioned, simply *the* measure against which one judges the worth of a life. Modernity, on the other hand, has questioned these traditional frameworks—consider the status of religion or family honor or patriotism as self-evident goods—rendering some obsolete, others highly contested, resulting in the sense that no framework could ever be considered *the* framework of morality.[64]

The fragility of the frameworks results in the sense that respect for other persons involves respecting their capacity to "express and develop their own opinions, to define their own life conceptions, to draw up their own life-plans."[65] So reoriented is the conception of self that at least part of the modern understanding of respect for others includes the capacity of each person to recognize the fragility of frameworks and to develop "an *individualized* identity, one that is particular to me, and that I dis-

---

62. Smith, *Taylor*, 93.

63. Taylor, *Sources of the Self*, 14–15.

64. Ibid., 16–17; cf. Taylor, *Secular Age*, 146–58.

65. Ibid., 25.

cover in myself. This notion arises along with an ideal, that of being true to myself and my own particular way of being," which is authenticity.[66]

While particular frameworks are contingent and historical, frameworks are necessary, for human agents are inextricably linked to strong values and have no identity without an interpreted relation to the good. For Taylor, this is an ontological thesis—without a moral dimension, human agency would be impossible, so humans cannot but be oriented to the good, or at least a stance towards the good:

> ... the claim is that living within such strongly qualified horizons is constitutive of human agency, that stepping outside these limits would be tantamount to stepping outside what we would recognize as integral, that is, undamaged human personhood ... To know who I am is a species of knowing where I stand. My identity is defined by the commitments and identifications which provide the frame or horizon within which I can try to determine from case to case what is good, or valuable, or what ought to be done, or what I endorse or oppose. In other words, it is the horizon within which I am capable of taking a stand.[67]

The notion of a horizon in which to take a stand is interesting. There might be a tendency to read the language of "taking a stand" as if it means "standing up for something," which it may on occasion mean, but it generally means something more basic. Much like perception occurs within a clearing of significance, so too do human agents occupy "moral space," in which they navigate their decisions, evaluate the worth of their desires and actions, form an identity, and even, perhaps, stand up for something.[68] Moral space is a basic ontological reality for humans, and to be without space, or to lose it, would be to "not know who one is," or even to not be anyone, to lack selfhood.[69] Borrowing from Merleau-Ponty's account of perception, Taylor articulates the absolute necessity of horizons from which to orient one's being:

> Our perceptual field has an orientational structure, a foreground and a background, an up and down. And it must have; that is, it can't lose this structure without ceasing to be a perceptual field in the full sense, our opening onto a world. In those rare moments

66. Taylor, *Multiculturalism*, 28.
67. Ibid., 27; cf. Smith, *Taylor*, 88.
68. Ibid., 29.
69. Ibid.

where we lose orientation, we don't know where we are; and we
don't know where or what things are either; we lose the thread of
the world . . . the confused debris into which our normal grasp
on things crumbles.[70]

Assuming that a person was free of moral horizons, or frameworks
of strong values, as if they took a view from nowhere with a head empty
of pre-judgments, would not result in a perfectly rational and enlight-
ened person, but rather "an appalling identity crisis," a person with "no
orientation," even "pathological."[71]

We cannot be intelligible without horizons of meaning, although
we do experience moments where meaning threatens to crumble into
nothingness along with our identities. Moral space is neither fixed nor
static, and just as selfhood was not understood by Taylor as a metaphysical property, neither is the unity of selfhood; still, while our identities
change there is a unity to the narrative of ourselves.[72] Unlike the disengaged subject of Descartes or the punctual self of Locke, we are not
able to view ourselves from above, so to speak, or from the vantage
point of eternity, and see with clarity and certainty the self and identity
we are.[73]Instead, we grasp ourselves as having a direction, aware that a
meaningful life is a good to be pursued, aware that there is a narrative
unity to our various projects and purposes, even when they change over
time. But we do all this from *within* our narrations and self-interpretations, from within our coming to terms with the world. Taylor insists
that our viewpoint is "essentially that of an embodied agent, engaged
with or at grips with the world" whereby we make sense of ourselves.[74]

Determining which good to seek, and how to interpret our own
selves in light of the changing goods to which we are devoted, is a matter
of practical reasoning and not the rule-following of universal criteria;
there is no better "measure of reality . . . in human affairs than those
terms which on critical reflection and after correction of errors we
detect make the best sense of our lives . . . not only offering the best,
most realistic orientation about the good but also allowing us best to
understand and make sense of the actions and feeling of ourselves and

---

70. Taylor, *Philosophical Arguments*, 23.

71. Ibid., 31.

72. Smith, *Taylor*, 97–98.

73. Taylor, *Sources of the Self*, 143–76.

74. Taylor, *Philosophical Arguments*, 23.

others."[75] The best account standard is less about what is necessary and more about how to become what we wish to be.

Key to this internal development are what Taylor refers to as hypergoods, "incomparably more important than others . . . the standpoint from which these must be weighted, judged, and decided about."[76] Given the potential conflicts of our desires, as well as the development of ourselves and our projects, frameworks tend to a terminus in a higher order good against which all other goods are judged or ranked—there is something, or perhaps several—of "overriding importance."[77] Generally, this good provides the direction of a life, and while there are many values and strong evaluations, many judgments of better or worse to be made between competing goods, "the one highest good has a special place. It is orientation to this which comes closest to defining my identity, and therefore my direction to this good is of unique importance to me. Whereas I naturally want to be well placed in relation to all and any of the goods I recognize and to be moving towards rather than away from them, my direction in relation to this good has a crucial importance."[78] Movement towards this good brings with it a sense of a good life, fullness; failure to attain, or to live up to this good calls for judgment and a sense of meaninglessness, however many of the other, lesser goods are attained.

Naturalism clouds understanding of hypergoods, says Taylor, both in assuming that our grasp should "neutralize our own anthropocentric reactions" so that our moral intuitions, purposes, and meanings are ignored or exorcized in keeping with some objective moral criteria, and by assuming that conflicting accounts of hypergoods could be made commensurable by the appropriate methodological procedures.[79] Instead, argues Taylor, hypergoods are identified precisely by what *means* to us, what *moves* us in our biographical narrative towards a sense of wholeness, significance, or authenticity. Nor is it beneficial to conceive of hypergoods as transcending human experience—the way that some might think of the moral significance of God or the Good—for hypergoods are elements of *our* horizons, our life projects and hermeneutics. This is not

75. Taylor, *Sources of the Self*, 56.
76. Ibid., 62–75.
77. Ibid., 62.
78. Ibid., 63.
79. Ibid., 73.

to say that there is not a God or a Good or an Ultimate Value, but it is to say that (1) one does not start with that value as an external criterion and deduce to conclusions of what is to be done, or (2) that higher goods are independent of our horizons. If they were utterly independent, they would be for us nothing, just as we would be utterly perplexed and disoriented without them, for engaged agency operates from within our stance to the world of value and from within our attempts to evaluate who we are, and how to come to grips with it all.[80]

Hypergoods do not compel because of their deductive force but because we experience "being *moved*."[81] Even when we glide along in obedience to authority or tradition without ourselves understanding or feeling the moral sources of the authority, we grasp that the founders were moved, and we trust their own compulsion, but in any event, hypergoods, the focal point of moral horizons and personal identities, are grounded in our strongest cares and concerns, our loves:

> We sense in every experience of being moved by some higher good that we are moved by what is good in it rather than that it is valuable because of our reaction. We are moved by it seeing its point as something infinitely valuable. We experience our love for it as a well-founded love. Nothing that couldn't move me in *this* way would count as a hypergood.[82]

To those bewitched by naturalism, Taylor claims, this cannot sound like anything other than subjectivism. He disagrees, claiming instead that his hermeneutics of engagement reveals an inescapable moral ontology, just as it reveals a normative element to authenticity, namely that the authentic subject loves what is deemed valuable. The rabid individualism feared by the moralists is in essence self-defeating because it knowingly makes insignificant (and thus incapable of the power to move) the terminus of the frameworks of identity, rendering the entire framework insignificant, and utterly perplexing. Just as a perceiver without a perceptual field was completely disoriented, and the self without a framework incoherent and pathological, so too would narcissism with respect to hypergoods erase the source of personal identity and worth, rendering the self utterly insignificant: "Which issues are significant,

80. Braman, *Meaning and Authenticity*, 36–37.
81. Taylor, *Sources of the Self*, 73.
82. Ibid.

I do not determine. If I did, no issue would be significant. But then the very ideal of self-choosing *as a moral ideal* would be impossible."[83] Authenticity cannot be defended, he claims, by collapsing horizons of significance, and even the sense that our own self-determination is utterly important, "depends on the understanding that *independent of my will* there is something noble, courageous, and hence significant in giving shape to my own life."[84] Certainly it is the case that degraded forms of self-fulfillment may be trivial and narcissistic, but authenticity depends upon a turn to the subject which "decenters inwardness" in self-transcendence:[85]

> ... I can define my identity only against the background of things that matter. But to bracket out history, nature, society, the demands of solidarity, everything but what I find in myself, would be to eliminate all candidates for what matters. Only if I exist in a world in which history, or the demands or nature, or the needs of my fellow human beings, or the duties of citizenship, or the call of God, or something else of this order *matters* crucially, can I define an identity for myself that is not trivial. Authenticity is not the enemy of demands that emanate from beyond the self; it supposes such demands.[86]

Authenticity demands values transcending the subject, which move the subject by being worthwhile, but not as some distant object proffering rules or demanding servile acquiescence. Instead, authenticity involves "being true to ourselves, but defining who we are as selves first involves being engaged by transcendent realities so that our self-interpretations might be informed by these sources."[87]

Of course, given his phenomenology, Taylor considers humans always already involved with the world of value, it is not as if the turn to the subject traps us behind a veil of ideas in some atomistic monad—there is no agent not already operating within a background and foreground of their cares and concerns, no self not already formed by a biography and a narrative of their own projects alongside others, history, and tradition. A thorough-going turn to the subject is a turn to the other, it is a

83. Taylor, *Ethics of Authenticity*, 39.
84. Ibid.
85. Plants, "Decentering Inwardness," 13–32.
86. Taylor, *Ethics of Authenticity*, 40–41.
87. Plants, "Decentering Inwardness," 16.

decentered self. The bogeyman of the modern subject, like most bogey-men, does not exist, nor could it ever exist, except in imagination. The problem with the subjective turn of modernity was that it turned only to mental space rather than to authentic subjectivity. In a thorough-going turn one discovers intentionality, and thus love, which carries the subject into the world, with and for others, and into that which has value. The opponents of authenticity fear that authenticity requires "repudiation of qualitative distinctions, a rejection of constitutive goods as such" but fail to recognize that freedom and authenticity are themselves "reflections of qualitative distinctions and presuppose some conception of qualitative goods."[88] For Taylor, subjectivity is not enlarged "at the expense of otherness . . . responsibility for the Other is integrated into the structure of selfhood. . . ."[89]

CONCLUSION

In the Introduction we cited with approval J. Donald Monan's claim that liberal education properly understood would be oriented towards the formation of the care for value. He says as well, "the critical test of human fulfillment and of liberal education is of the same order: It is no mere question of speculative knowing or not knowing, but it is a question either of richness or of emptiness of life."[90] In the chapters since, we have developed the outlines of a creative retrieval of a philosophical anthropology rooted in love, claiming that this anthropology is evident, admittedly with various levels of sophistication and methodical clarity, by Plato, Augustine, Aquinas, Heidegger, and Taylor. To be sure, despite their political and civil concerns, the anthropology in Plato, Augustine, and Aquinas is perhaps more about mind than sociality, and we read Heidegger and Taylor as providing needed developments for the tradition of inwardness. The inner turn bereft of the hermeneutics of facticity and engagement can indeed sink into the veil of ideas entrapping the disengaged, disembodied, punctual self, even into the excesses of self-indulgent narcissism feared by the opponents of authenticity. So the tradition of inwardness develops its account of love to grasp its engagement with the world of value, meaning, and self-transcendence.

88. Taylor, *Sources of the Self*, 98.

89. Smith, *Taylor*, 113.

90. Monan, "Value Proposition."

Still, it seems to us that the figures examined thus far have not yet adequately articulated the structures of intentionality.[91] The tradition first performed intentionality analysis (Plato, Augustine, Aquinas) before reflecting on it explicitly (Heidegger and Taylor), but the structure of intentionality is not fully articulated, neither are the concrete effects of sin and grace. Given the background of the previous chapters, we turn for the remainder of the book to the thought of Bernard Lonergan, albeit in conversation with others, to provide the detailed structure of intentionality needed for the normative fullness of authenticity, to understand the role of conversion, to grasp the effects of sin and grace on the performance of love, and to grasp the full directedness of value and love. Only with a threefold conversion—intellectual, moral, and religious—is authenticity fully redeemed and subjectivity fully engaged.

91. See Plants, "Decentering Inwardness," 14. See also his "Lonergan and Taylor," 143–72.

3

Bernard Lonergan, Intellectual Conversion, and Authentic Love

Perhaps more than any other thinker, Bernard Lonergan is able to appropriate from the past and the present. He develops sophisticated readings of Augustine and Aquinas, in conversation with Kant and Heidegger, to provide a phenomenology of the concrete subject based in the primacy of the human subject as a loving, desiring being. From this account Lonergan derives a full vision of human knowing, being, and acting that would guide education in its cultural, civilizational, and transformational aspirations. Augustine, Aquinas, Heidegger, Taylor, and Lonergan provide a vision of the human being as lover, and this vision gives a normative task to Christian education. But, of course, this integral vision is disrupted by sin.

WHAT IS TRUTH?

For a university to be a university, it must wrestle with the question of truth. Yet it seems more natural today to ask, "Whose truth?" rather than to speak of "the truth." And there are good reasons for this. Relativism does not merely spring from decades of advertisement-laden media saturation and the doublespeak of political spin-doctors. The question arises from our everyday experience of finding out how differently our neighbors think of things. Anyone who has ever been immersed in a cross-cultural situation will likely testify to the disorienting experience of having one's intuitions and assumptions be largely wrong. And in today's university, the cross-cultural experience may well come from our neighbors.

The modern philosophical tradition further complicates the question of truth. Immanuel Kant's *Critique of Pure Reason*, probably the most influential philosophical work of the last two centuries, argues that we have no knowledge of reality as it is in itself, but only of reality as it is perceived.[1] Many of the relativistic understandings of truth, adverted to above, knowingly or unknowingly draw on Kant's legacy. But if truth does not concern reality as it is, what remains of the value of the term? But how can a university be a university without teaching about reality?

Bernard Lonergan offers an analysis of this quandary that acknowledges the brilliance and challenges of modern philosophy but which locates the real problem at a much deeper level. According to Lonergan, human beings are naturally beset, based on the type of being that they are, by a persistent and stubborn myth about knowledge. Much modern philosophical training exacerbates this myth. While it is possible to outgrow the myth in a fairly natural progression of human development, overcoming it in a stable and integral way will likely require a radical clarification of our understanding of human knowing.

AUGUSTINE'S DILEMMA

The perennial nature of this struggle can be seen in the intellectual and spiritual pilgrimage of Augustine, already adverted to in this book. In his *Confessions*, he wrestles most of all with the question of who (and what) is the true God.[2] Perhaps Augustine's main point, as he tells his life story in the *Confessions*, is that in order to know himself he must first know God. And knowing God involves knowing reality, for to know God above all means to know the truth.

In the course of his conversion, Augustine comes up against a very peculiar kind of problem. He wants to believe in God, who is good and incorruptible, but is blocked from this by his conception of God as a body. Even as a very fine kind of light, suffusing all creation—the highest kind of body Augustine could imagine—how could a body truly be incorruptible and good? Every body is subject to motion and change. And if God's being suffuses all reality, why does it not drive evil out? But

---

1. See Kant, *Critique of Pure Reason*; it was not Kant's intention to spawn epistemic relativism—quite the opposite—but there is many a slip 'twixt the cup and the lip.

2. See Augustine, *Confessions, passim.*

if God is not a body—without form, without shape, without dimension, without color or shade—is God anything at all? Is God really there?

BEYOND ANIMAL KNOWING

As Lonergan analyzes this dilemma, he believes that Augustine's problems stem from the deep ambivalence within us between animalistic ways of knowing reality, which are most spontaneous for us, and fully human ways of knowing reality, which we must achieve. As animals, we interact with the world as we encounter it and as it is useful to us. Therefore it is perfectly natural for us to seek "bodies": external components of reality that are present and available for us. And we are right to do so, for that which is already out there now, available for us to see or grasp, is essential for us a living, animal beings.[3] Yet to interact with reality only in this way, Lonergan argues, is to miss out on the fully human way of knowing reality that, provoked by wonder, goes beyond mere interaction with bodies.[4]

The basis of the myth, Lonergan argues, is that we are both animal beings and something more. And it is easy to confuse the criteria for knowledge in the animal world with that of the higher, spiritual and intellectual, aspects of our being. In Augustine's long-fought victory to know God intellectually, and not as a body, Lonergan sees an authentic person following the lead of wonder to achieve truly human knowing.

When we are following the myth, we assume knowing to be something understandable by an analogy with ocular vision. In other words, "reality" is something we encounter, and knowing reality means to have a direct, or unimpeded, encounter with it. By analogy, we know something when we can see it clearly and distinctly, or (to move to another sensory analogy) when we can have direct contact with it.[5]

This type of knowing does match up quite well with what it means to be a successful animal. Sensitive animal existence has most concern

3. For example, what feeds me is the plate of spaghetti, hot and tasty, present now for me on the table, available for me to stick my fork into. As an animal being, what is important about reality for me is that which is externally present, independent of me, and available for my use.

4. Lonergan, *Insight: A Study of Human Understanding*, 22.

5. See the discussion of space and time in Lonergan, *Insight*, 163–95, for an explanation of this type of knowing and of the necessity for progressing beyond its valid but limited viewpoint.

for objects as it is able to eat or mate with them, or as they present threats. What the robin cares about, within the limits of its animal psychology, is the worm as a body: present, out-there now, available to eat. Or, during mating season, it cares about the robin of the opposite gender; and at all times the snake slithering toward it is of concern. The idea of the snake and the intellectual appropriation of the worm are not biologically useful. That which is "out there now" is.

KNOWING BEING

With respect to this animal aspect of presence and usefulness, the idea or intelligibility can seem to be something distinct from and derivative of the really real bodily presence of the thing. What interests me is the food, mate, or threat that is "really out there." The idea of the thing, on the contrary, is more nebulous. From this viewpoint, it can seem to reside "in my head."

Knowing an object, then, would seem to mean abstracting an adequate idea of it from experiencing the reality of the thing. For example, truly to know the plate of spaghetti that I am about to eat means to have formed an adequate idea of it based on my encounter with it. I would know it if in fact it is the plate of spaghetti I think it is, and not a cleverly disguised pile of string or worms.

In this paradigm, objectivity amounts to unimpeded contact, or direct encounter, of a thing. Again the analogy of ocular vision is instructive. If we can see something clearly and distinctly, we have an unimpeded presence of the thing to us. We know it objectively because we have a true view of it. Subjectivity creeps in when either we are unable to see the thing clearly, or when some aspect of our vision keeps us from encountering it as it really is out there.

Kant's *Critique of Pure Reason* devastatingly attacks exactly this understanding of knowledge. As he cogently argues, our perceiving of a thing is not an act distinct from us who are doing the perceiving, but is a creative act in itself. Therefore, when we are speaking of encounter with reality, we are more properly speaking not of the reality that is encountered but of our experience of it. For what we have direct access to are our perceptions. Because Kant agreed with this notion of knowledge, he concluded that humans have no objective knowledge of reality.[6] There

6. See Kant's discussion of the transcendental aesthetic in the *Critique of Pure Reason* for a discussion of space and time on these terms. Kant did believe that we have

is no unimpaired view of objects, because our perception itself must be accounted for as a limiting factor.

According to Lonergan, a deep similarity exists between this notion of knowledge, which Kant both espouses and problematizes, and the notion of God as a body, which Augustine struggled to overcome. In both cases, reality is something "already out there now." Augustine's breakthrough came when he realized that the presence and reality of God has more the character of a truth that is known than the character of a body that is encountered.[7]

To know a truth means to know a meaning, and the reality of the thing known is mediated to us through that meaning. Truth and meaning are not limited (or even describable) in spatial terms, as bodies are. They can mediate spatial reality to us, but themselves are neither intrinsically "in here" nor "out there." What Augustine discovered is that with respect to the reality he was trying to know (the highest reality, that of God), he would be successful not by finding God somewhere out there, but by contemplating the meanings that mediated God's being to him. In this way, the criterion for knowing reality is not the directness of our encounter with it but the correctness of the meanings that mediate being to us.

The world as known by a successful animal is real and important, but it is only a fragment of the world known in a fully human way. The myth that human knowledge is so easily subject to is that all knowing must conform to the criteria of animalistic knowing. But when human beings speak of the real world, they mean a world far wider than animalistic knowing-by-encounter can explain.

The real world, as we almost always mean it, is a world mediated to us by sets of meanings and partially constituted by meanings. It includes mathematical, physical, chemical, biological, psychological, intellectual and spiritual aspects of reality. Within it are such things as triangles, momentum, oxygen, trees, cats, families, and prayer. All of these realities have meaning and intelligibility as a basic component. In other words, their meanings are not extrinsic add-ons, applied to the underlying reality of things, which underlying true reality and being may or may not be

---

objective knowledge of these perceptions, and he attributed the certainty achieved in mathematics and the natural sciences to this objectivity. Things as they are in themselves, however, are unknown to us.

7. Augustine, *Confessions*, Book 7.

knowable to us. Rather, the reality of things—their being—is known by and through those sets of meanings.

Take, for example, the reality of a family. If reality conforms to the expectations of animalistic knowing, does a family exist? Where is it? One can encounter the individual people, but look as we might, no family will be found. It would seem that "family" is just a concept in our minds that we use to group the really existing people. But when we speak of the real world, we often especially mean the world in which we have relationships and responsibilities, such as a family. In fully human knowing, as Lonergan explains it, families have real existence. They are intelligible realities that one can know by following the drive of wonder and asking and answering questions. They are not bodies in the external world that one can find. But the point is that by knowing families we know something true, an aspect of the real world mediated to us through meanings.

As opposed to a family, something like oxygen would seem to have a different status in terms of being known and really existing. After all, oxygen is "really out there now." You can find it, grasp it, and encounter it. There is, of course, a difference. A family is composed of human acts of meaning; our understandings, judgments, and subsequent decisions and actions constitute the reality of it. Oxygen is not constituted of human acts of meaning in the same way.

And yet, oxygen, in its being and existence, is mediated to us (known by us) through human acts of meaning. No one knows oxygen by direct encounter alone. We encounter the pressure and bodily need for air, yet for most of human existence we had no knowledge that a special element called oxygen existed. Joseph Priestly deduced its existence in 1774, and Antoine Lavoisier gave its current name to it in 1777. The closest any human can currently come to directly grasping oxygen, perhaps, would be in the readouts of an electron microscope. In this case, a number of scans of the distortion of electron wavelengths are averaged to correlate to an image that would correspond to what we would see in visual light.

But this is not the way we really know oxygen. We know it in its relation to other elements on the periodic table. We know it in its relation to acts of combustion (the way Lavoisier was able to know and name it, disproving an earlier theory of how combustion occurs). We know it in the bars of color it produces in a visible spectrum analysis, related to other sets of color bars produced by other elements. We do know it through the readouts of the electron microscope, but we know it therein as it is related to aspects of visible light and to the way other elements' readouts are correlated to visible light. We know it in the life-giving function oxygen has for animal life. In other words we know the being of oxygen through sets of meanings that mediate its being to us. When Priestly and Lavoisier made their breakthrough discoveries, we knew the truth about a new aspect of reality. The meanings are therefore not add-ons; rather, we know the real being of oxygen through them; the real being of oxygen is an intelligible reality.

The mediation of being through human acts of meaning in such realities as families and oxygen can help us understand the way we know other realities that we can grasp and feel. What are we doing when we know something we seemingly can grasp, such as the family cat? Is it really the case that the "stuff" of the cat—the base materials of the fur and claws, flesh and bones—is the reality of the cat, and the ideas we have about the cat are add-ons that we supply? Conversely, are those ideas all that are worth talking about as a "cat," in some way independent of, or unknowably related to, the real being of the cat?

In either of these cases, we have to ignore some data about the cat, ruling irrelevant significant insights that we actually do have and function with. One of the scientific names for a cat is *felix domesticus*. Indicated in that name is a significant relation by which we know what it is that we are talking about: a connection with our home, or *domus*. This connection places the cat also relative to non-domesticated species of cats. Whether or not a particular *felix domesticus* is in fact domesticated, it is the kind of cat that often does become incorporated into human society. Other species of cats (for example, *wild*cats or cougars) would become so only sporadically. The argument is not that human society has changed the being of *felix domesticus*, putting its mark upon it (although it has). The point is that we know something significant about the cat in terms of its ability to form a part of our societies and the actuality of its regularly doing so.

The reality of the family cat, as with the rest of the real world, is mediated to us through sets of meanings. These meanings are commonly (and perhaps always) known as sets of relations to other realities we know in the world. The cat is an animal, related to other animals such as bears, butterflies, and barracudas. The cat is domesticated, related in ways that can be specified to a particular aspect of human society, to other domesticated animals, and to non-domesticated animals. The cat is a mammal and a fairly strict carnivore, placing it in relation to other sets of living beings and eating practices. A particular cat might be a family's cat, placing it in particular reference to a set of human beings. These sets of meanings are not merely add-ons that we supply, nor are they disconnected from the being of the cat. Rather we know the reality of the cat through these sets of relations. In some cases, the sets of relations are constituted by human acts of meaning, in some cases human acts of meaning discover them.[8]

CRITERIA OF OBJECTIVITY

One can thereby see that the criteria of objectivity for the world mediated by meaning (the real world, known humanly) differ markedly from those of the world of merely animalistic knowing. In the world of merely animalistic knowing, immediate presence is the hallmark of objectivity. Can you grab it, see it, and experience it in a direct and unimpeded way? In the world mediated by meaning (that is, in the real world), experience is still present and basic, and it must be truly attentive to the reality experienced. Experience is only a start, however, for on the basis of our experiences, we wonder. The path of genuine knowledge follows that wonder.

Objectivity thereby comes to mean being authentic to your experiences and yourself as an inquirer. Do we ask questions about our experience and form concepts that meet its exigencies, intelligently considered? Do we assess those concepts reasonably, assessing which of them, if any, are supported by evidence? Do we come to a grasp of sufficient evidence (either probably or certainly) to warrant assent that one of those conceptions is actually the case?

When we follow through with the call of wonder, culminating in the real gift of self in love, we are true to the basic character of our being. Lonergan, therefore, named four "transcendental precepts:" be attentive, be intelligent, be reasonable, be responsible.[9] Obeying these precepts means following through with the immanent norms of our own

---

8. For a more technical discussion of human knowing, see Snell, *Though a Glass Darkly.*

9. See Lonergan, *Method*, 20, 53, and 55.

experiencing, understanding, judging, and deciding being. Failing to do so means to fail to be who we really are. In his account of human knowing and deciding, Lonergan does not neglect the results of human acts of cognition—they are obviously crucial—but especially wants to show what it means for the process of human cognition to go right. The transcendental precepts explain what that procedural rightness is; and, that rectitude consists not of buckling under to an external standard (though there may be legitimate external standards) but rather giving free reign to the requirements of the ongoing motion and action of our own being when we seek to know and love.

By following the lead of wonder—attentively, intelligently, reasonably—we can come to correct understandings of the experiences that we have. And in coming to correct understandings, we come to knowledge of the world. For the real world is mediated to us not by encounter alone but by the meanings through which we explain the reality that we encounter.[10]

Lonergan calls the transition from more animalistic ways of knowing to fully human knowing, which Augustine made with respect to knowledge of God, "intellectual conversion" or "intellectual self-transcendence."[11] It is expected to occur naturally as humans come to adulthood. However, the character of this spontaneous conversion is unstable; true virtue is not accidental, but must be earned. It is especially vulnerable to the course of philosophical study. As he says:

> It occurs spontaneously when one reaches the age of reason, implicitly drops earlier criteria of reality (Are you awake? Do you see it? Is it heavy? etc.), and proceeds to operate on the criteria of sufficient evidence or sufficient reason. But this spontaneous conversion is insecure. The use of the earlier criteria can recur. It is particularly likely to recur when one gets involved in philosophic issues. For then the objectification of what is meant by sufficient evidence or sufficient reason may become exceedingly complex, while the objectification of getting a good look is simplicity itself.[12]

10. See the chapter on "Self-Affirmation of the Knower" in Lonergan, *Insight*, 343–71.

11. Lonergan, *Method in Theology*, 114; see also Lonergan, "Self-Transcendence: Intellectual, Moral, Religious."

12. Lonergan, "Unity and Plurality," 248.

In knowing the real world through inquiry and a grasp of sufficient evidence, one comes to adulthood in terms of what it means to know the world. One has rejected (either explicitly or implicitly) the myth that knowing the world is constituted by encounter alone and come to terms with the objectivity that comes from a grasp of sufficient reason. If this transition happens in a thorough and stable way, one has radically clarified the human relation to truth.[13]

The concern persists that knowledge which may be wrong cannot rightly be described as knowledge (or, what is to say the same thing, as objectively valid). We are finite beings, and even our most intelligent and reasonable affirmations cannot preclude the possibility of further relevant questions someday arising. Authenticity is good, but does it really measure up as a criterion for what objective knowing is supposed to be?

To put it bluntly, it seems that under Lonergan's analysis, objective human knowing can sometimes be wrong. The criteria of authenticity do not produce the kind of apodictic certainty we desire. If something might not be true, how can one claim to know it? Are we not claiming that sometimes a person has knowledge but is in fact wrong? And is that not a contradiction in terms?[14]

Our answer is we are trying to understand human knowing, and that infallible knowing does not seem to be a merely human possibility. By claiming an infallible truth, one is claiming the kind of permanence of judgment that cannot ever be changed. But the affirmation, "Heaven and earth may pass away, but my judgment will never pass away," is not a statement that we believe can rightly be made on merely human terms. It is, in fact, to claim the knowledge of a god.

To hold human knowledge to that standard would be to say that in order to know something, a human must become a god. It seems to me that Kant (and Nietzsche) both do hold humans to that standard. Because human knowing cannot measure up to that standard, it is therefore nothing, or at least a radically limited thing with respect to knowing the real world. But the fact that we have built civilizations (or that we can

13. For a readable explanation of Lonergan's project by one of his first students, see Flanagan, *Quest for Self-Knowledge*.

14. Mortimer Adler puts the expectation this way: "Opinions can be true or false. Opinions can be right or wrong. We all recognize this, I think. But think a moment, knowledge can't be false, knowledge can't be wrong. If something is knowledge it's impossible for it to be false knowledge or wrong knowledge." Adler, *How to Think About the Great Ideas*, 14.

have this particular argument at all) seems to me to testify to the validity of human forms of knowing.

The right foundation of fully human knowledge, then, is humility. Knowledge on fully human terms (but conversely, on merely human terms) must admit that its judgments are not certain in the way a divine pronouncement is. Fully human knowledge resolutely claims that in correct understanding we know the real world. But it is still we, we finite ones, we human ones, that are doing the knowing. Our knowing is valid, but we have not yet come to complete knowledge of the universe. Being authentic to ourselves as questioners means including this confident but humble awareness in all our answers.

THOMAS ON WISDOM AND CHARITY

Even if one accepts what we have described as "fully human knowing" as valid, however, significant questions can remain as to whether our actual human cognitional process matches up to the criteria of objectivity given above. Are we in fact ever attentive, intelligent, reasonable, and responsible in a way that yields valid knowledge of the world? What guarantees that we will live up to our part of the bargain?

When Thomas Aquinas considered the problem of knowing reality, the widest terms under which he did so were those of wisdom. Wisdom, in Thomas' understanding, might be called the habit of reality. That is, wisdom is able to assess both the correctness of one's knowledge of the world (Is what I know about the world really true?) and the rectitude of one's processes of knowing the world (Am I knowing the world in the right way?).[15] The wise person is the one who can get knowledge right in both these ways. While wisdom does therefore boil down to a kind of knowledge, it is a regulating kind. It has not so much connected with specific inquiries as to the relation of the whole and the rightness of the knower with respect to that whole.

In that light, it is striking that Thomas so strongly connects wisdom with love. While charity (the supernatural gift of love) is the form of all the virtues, wisdom specifically springs from charity.[16] In other words, because the saved person has received the gift of friendship with God, he is able to know God's creation on different, more realistic, terms. He

15. *ST* II-II 45.6.
16. *ST* II-II 45.6 *re. ad.* 2.

does not necessarily become an expert in any aspect of human knowledge, but is in fact better able to judge the adequacy of human knowing because he is connected in friendship with the source of all and orderer of the whole.

But why would love make such a difference for knowledge? Knowing seems to be one thing, while loving seems to be another; we can even refer to love as "blind." It seems one could be a deeply loving person, but still not very knowledgeable. While Thomas' connection of wisdom and charity seems attractive, will it not fall short of answering the questions with which we started? For it seems that love, as we ordinarily conceive it, is a poor tool to guarantee the correctness of our knowledge of the world.

The answer to these questions begins with the insight that reason—the way we know the world—is not an instrument or tool that we use, but rather it is we, ourselves, as we interact genuinely with the world. Furthermore, neither is love a tool; it is we, our self-transcendent selves, as we live in openness and friendship toward the world. Thomas did not have a modern, instrumental, view of reason and love. He saw them as integral to the operations of our being.

HEIDEGGER ON SELVES AND WORLD

As we have already discussed, one of the most powerful modern opponents of the instrumental view of reason and love is the German philosopher Martin Heidegger. To understand the way we can appropriate Thomas' insight within the modern context, it will be helpful to review an aspect of Heidegger's work. In particular, his notions of Care and Mood serve as useful ways to interpret and understand the validity of Thomas' linking of wisdom and charity.[17]

Heidegger, again, argues that successfully to understand our existence we will need to take note of the way we are always already within a linguistically and culturally charged historical setting. Within this context, our existence has the character of an event. We are present within this context in an active way, and in fact, we are more successful in understanding our existence if we see this active and situated "Being-There"

---

17. See Thiselton, *Two Horizons*, 192, on the ontological status of mood (or State-of-Mind) in both Tillich and Heidegger.

as intrinsic to who we are.[18] In other words, the nature of our identity is not that of a static substance, considered abstractly and disconnected from a world, but our very existence involves Being-in-the-World.

As those whose being is "Being-There," and "Being-in-the World," existence has the character of a challenge and a risk. The challenge of our existence is to become and find our true identity. Because we are enmeshed in a world, the character of the world always has the potential to cover over our own true selves. We can become lost in purposeless activity, in idle chatter, in sets of meanings and values that are not our own but are merely absorbed by us. Hence the risk that instead of becoming authentic selves we will lose ourselves to the crowd, to the average everydayness of routine and purposeless activity.

For our world is a set of relations, and these relations are not extrinsic to us but constitutive of our selves. The tasks and purposes we have constitute the nature of our event, our Being-There. Heidegger characterizes human existence as "essentially teleological; in each of our actions we express goals which point outward to some sense of our lives as a final, definitive configuration of meaning. . . . I make a commitment, whether consciously or not, concerning my overview of what my life amounts to as a totality—concerning what kind of person I am."[19] This commitment both characterizes and constitutes our being.

The fundamental constitutive aspect of human existence, then, is care, or concern. Our values and motivation indicate and convey concern, and they indicate the way that our existence is enmeshed in a world revealed to us by that concern. Care, or concern, gives substance and direction to our existence. In a way, it is our existence. For who and what we really are—the nature of our event—becomes manifest in the way that interest and value move us. The aspects of the world that do not connect to us through concern, in a real way, are not really "the world" for us. But in the purposes we have in life, revealed and existing in the care that we have, we truly have a world and become alive in it.

By care, as we have already explained, Heidegger means much more than individual instances of concern. The shape of our lives is set by care. The analysis of care reveals to us that have a basic underlying "mood," or orientation, according to which we respond to the world and

18. Besides Heidegger's own work, which we have already referred to, see also Braman, *Meaning and Authenticity*, 8–17.

19. Guignon, "Heidegger's 'Authenticity' Revisited," 331.

that orders the rest of our concern. Our affective being has a shape, direction, or contour that indicates the basic attitude we have toward the world. Are we open and receptive to new encounters, seeking the truth whatever form it might take? Do we close ourselves off, admitting the value of only a restricted portion of the world of being? These questions, and their answers, convey the way that we are able to relate to the world in which we are enmeshed. One could even refer to "mood" —this underlying affective orientation—as an 'ontological disposition' in which the event of our being is constituted by the overall shape of our concern.[20]

Far from being a factor in our lives or a tool we use, then, charity turns out to speak to the constitution of our very selves. For charity, in Aquinas' terms, is first of all a habit—an ontological disposition—that forms the basis for the way we bring our existence into actuality. As beings constituted by enmeshment in a world, love finds a way for that enmeshment to be right, for our own true selves to be rightly related in this world.

TAYLOR ON SITUATED REASON

The Canadian philosopher Charles Taylor significantly develops Heidegger's basic insight on the way that we are selves by being part of a world. In *Being and Time*, Heidegger investigated his intuition of our enmeshment in a world—our Being-There—very thoroughly, but in a way that ultimately cuts us off from the self-transcendence we seek. The ultimate horizon of our being, of our world, is death; we are living most authentically when we realize and resolutely live toward our coming dissolution.[21] The "mood," or ontological disposition, Heidegger deals with is in fact a very dark thing: "keeping watch on the fire in the night," as he put it in a discourse to his students. Because he deals only with the self in terms of the categories of finitude and of what is available to us as enmeshed in this world, it is difficult to see any other ultimate end. Taylor, however, seeks to validate Heidegger's insight about our Being-in-a-World but to do so in a way that discovers sources for a self that truly is moral and self-transcendent. To situate Aquinas' affirmation of wisdom, we will also reexamine an aspect of Taylor's thought.

20. Braman, *Meaning and Authenticity*, 16, quoting Richardson, *Heidegger*, 34.
21. Heidegger, *Being and Time*, 299–311.

According to Taylor, the fact that we exist only as those who are enmeshed in a world means that we are ordered to an ultimate good. Because our lives have the character of an event, it is of intrinsic importance for us as selves whether our event is good, or whether it is lacking. But for our event to be good, we must be living unto some good, directed in the operation of our being toward a higher meaning or greater story.[22]

In patterning our lives after an ultimate good, we find the moral basis for who we truly are. To be a human person means to embrace the good. Taylor would argue that Heidegger is right in viewing death as a basic reality of the human situation. But Taylor would also argue that in making it the ultimate last word about the human situation, Heidegger has closed off further relevant questions. In Taylor's analysis, we actually find ourselves not by a concentration on our death, which can be narcissistic and closed off to others, but by our real and conscious connection to a greater good.[23]

The ultimate expression of this orientation toward the good is love.[24] Not every kind of good can order our lives, but only a good that is capable of being a genuine moral source. Some things, that are good in themselves, are only good because they are ordered to a higher way of life. Freedom, for example, is necessary for the good life but is only itself a good if its use is good. Our freedom can become an absolute evil if we choose to make it so. Freedom becomes a true good when it is actuated in righteous choices. But other kinds of good are ordering goods, the kinds of goods that reveal something of ultimate worth and that draw us to live in line with that. Of these, the highest is love, and in particular the love of God.

To be a self, then, means being a moral being. To be a moral being means that in the event of one's becoming that one is ordered to an ultimate good, a higher story that is capable of drawing one toward real self-transcendence. To be ordered to the highest good—the most authentic source of selfhood—means to be ordered in and by the love of God.

22. Braman, *Meaning and Authenticity*, 38.

23. See Taylor, *Sources of the Self*, 374–81, on the moral and self-constitutive aspect of what he calls the "expressivist turn."

24. Braman, *Meaning and Authenticity*, 39.

RELIGIOUS CONVERSION AS GROUNDING
INTELLECTUAL CONVERSION

The most significant question of our lives, according to Lonergan, is whether we have been captured by God's love. God's love provides the foundational situation for our living as rational beings. It also grounds the horizon within which we live, both providing for its possibility and orienting us within it to ultimate truth and goodness.[25]

Being captured by God's love, according to Lonergan, can best be understood in the categories of Christian spirituality. In the Ignatian tradition, the only secure basis for making a serious choice in life is the realization that one, oneself, has been chosen by God.[26] The mark of this divine election is the love one has toward God. Ignatius does not here mean the sincere but limited love prompted by divine gifts and prom-ises. Rather it is the way one finds oneself bound in love toward God in an unlimited way, in a way that is out of proportion to anything in this world to produce or satisfy. Whatever else we know, we know that we can never be the same. On the basis of this love, a love this world can-not provide or satisfy but only God himself, one can make choices that reflect the secure nature of one's place in God.

The love of God, itself the gift of God, places one in a horizon that is quite different from the loss-of-self implied by envelopment in average-everydayness. One's identity has changed because of loving in a way that one could not love before. One experiences a "universal anteced-ent willingness" to know what is real and choose what is good because openness and self-giving are natural to someone in love. By "natural," Lonergan does not mean "according to the usual run of things for the human species"; rather, the conscious operations of our knowing and choosing have become transformed because of the gift of God's love. In fact, we have begun to love in a way that is more natural for God than for us as a result of God's work within us.

Lonergan terms this most basic change "religious conversion."[27] It is a conversion in that it is a change of direction from sinful self-centered-

25. See Lonergan, *Understanding and Being: The Halifax Lectures on "Insight,"* 182. Lonergan's main discussion of horizon in *Method* is in the section, "Horizons," in the chapter "Dialectics." See Lonergan, *Method,* 235–37. See Lonergan, *Method,* 241, for religious conversion as constitutive of horizon.

26. Ignatius Loyola, *Spiritual Exercises,* 205; Lonergan, *Method,* 106.

27. Lonergan, *Method,* 240–41.

ness toward openness to all things (based on openness to, captivation by, God). It is religious in that it is the result of God's work in us. It does not necessarily imply adherence to any of the world's religious traditions. It does imply that one has been changed.

This change is expected by Lonergan to be conscious; it is an aspect of the operation of our consciousness. But that does not mean that this conscious change will be easily apprehended at any single moment. It may be "revealed in retrospect as an under-tow of existential conscious-ness, as a fated acceptance of a vocation to holiness, as perhaps an increasing simplicity and passivity in prayer."[28] The main criterion for religious conversion is not dramatic conversion events (at least, not in any required way) but the change in who one is and how one's conscious operations take place.

Such a transformation has clear ramifications for the nature of one's ethical being. To be oriented within a horizon toward God, the ultimate good, means also to be ordered with a transformed attitude regarding lesser goods (that is, all of the goods in the created world). One does not automatically become a more ethical being, but fundamental changes in one's moral nature have become more probable. Because the true nature of all other goods is to be subordinate to the ultimate Good, namely God, being ordered authentically to God empowers and moves one to live more authentically to the world God has made.[29]

How, though, does love order intellectual rectitude? The connection with moral transformation seems fairly direct. Love of God, truly having captured one's being, leads one naturally to love what God loves, or to love that which is like God because it bears the imprint of the Creator in its very being. But how does love situate intelligence, and why does this transformed horizon ground our ability to know truth in the world?

Knowledge, according to Lonergan, has an essentially moral char-acter. When we know, we are knowing the being of a thing and may also know its value. But as knowers, we are guided by ethical demands to be attentive to the data we try to understand, inquire and form possible answers to the questions we have in an intelligent way, and affirm or deny the adequacy of those answers reasonably. While the *content* of our knowing is something preliminary to making ethical choices, the *process* of pursuing knowledge is itself a series of ethical choices. For each of the

28. Ibid.
29. Ibid., 291.

conscious operations involved in knowing can be pursued in a way that is either authentic or unauthentic to ourselves as questioning beings and to the nature of the world we are trying to know.

The transformation of our whole conscious being described by religious conversion, therefore, makes more probable the radical clarification of the human process of knowing described above as intellectual conversion. While religious conversion in Lonergan's terms does not necessarily require adherence to any religion, we most authentically understand this transformation in religious terms. But religious doctrines mediate the being and value of the world to us through sets of meanings that we are asked to believe. In believing these meanings, to the extent that the religion in question is true, we know the real world.

Consider, for example, the words of Jesus on the Cross, "It is finished," set forth by the Evangelist in John 19. In Greek, the perfect tense of this declaration does not allow the ambiguity of the English phrase; *tetelestai*, the last word spoken by Jesus before his death, is a victory cry. It means that the goal has been accomplished and that its power endures still. But where, in something "already out there now" is the victory? Having said this word, Jesus breathed his last. Yet this victory declaration does communicate the reality of the Crucifixion. Despite the brutal wrong of the murder of Christ, the victory he sought to win through his incarnation was achieved. One only knows the events on Golgotha rightly if one knows those sets of meanings. In fact, it is by knowing those sets of meanings that one truly knows the death of Christ.

One does not have to be intellectually converted, of course, authentically to be part of a religious tradition in which one responds to and tries to understand one's religious conversion. But the way in which religious doctrines mediate to us the meaning and value of the world does set one up to overcome the myth that knowing is like seeing, that the world is known by us along the analogy of encounter. For the doctrines do not point simply to encounters. They interpret our encounters, giving meaning and value to human experience. The quest to understand what one has received by faith leads, therefore, to an openness to the radical clarification of human knowing that results from realizing what it means to know and to believe.

AUTHENTIC BEING AS BEING-IN-LOVE

Our existence as lovers, then, grounds our existence as choosers and knowers. To express our meaning more fully, the way that God's love has transformed us makes it more likely for us to value what is truly good and know that which is really real. This is so because God's love changes our conscious operations by changing us, the conscious operators. We become authentic knowers and choosers because we have become true to ourselves and true to the Creator of the world in which we know and choose through love.

Authentic Being-in-the-World, then, is Being-in-Love. For in love we are most true to the kinds of beings that we truly are. And the eyes of love, rather than being blind, situate us rightly with respect to the true values of the world. Love maximizes our reasonable being—that is, our knowing and choosing selves—because in love we follow the inner norms of our wonder most fully. Just as we discover and value the world most truly through love, in love we become most fully who we truly are. For the reality of our conscious selves is that we are led by wonder and motivated by the good.

I believe this explanation justifies Aquinas' confidence that the fullness of love effectively grounds the reality of our ability to know the world. Wisdom springs from charity; we habitually come to know the world because we have learned what it means to exist rightly in it. The actuality of love, therefore, grounds and ensures the authenticity of the conscious operations by which we follow wonder and know the truth. Rather than asking whether our minds are able to bridge the gap between ourselves and the world, then, the right question is whether we are rightly situated within the world. That is, do we truly follow the way of love?

However, with this realization in place, it may seem that we have only magnified the problem. It would seem that if a straightforward answer to this question, "Do we truly follow the way of love?" can be given, the answer would be, "No, we do not follow love, or at least not very well." For the reality of human sinfulness shouts to us the manifold nature of our corporate downfall. If we are to take seriously the nature of the love that grounds our knowledge of the truth, and thereby to come to see more clearly the nature of the Christian university's task, we will have to account for the nature of the sin that distorts both our willing and knowing being.

Part Two

Educating for Moral and Religious Conversion

4

Disorder and Revolt

The Effects of Sin

The totality of depravity includes the noetic effects of sin. In conversation with the Reformed tradition, we argue that Aquinas' vision of the noetic effects of sin, which he is often falsely accused of ignoring, provides a vital hint of how sin disrupts the intellect, and therefore education. Aquinas does not overlook sin, but gives a nuanced and sophisticated account much in keeping with the order of love; however, Aquinas is limited by his thirteenth century metaphysics and needs transposition into the language of phenomenology, which is done by Lonergan. Lonergan provides a thoroughgoing account of the way that biases distort the functioning of our consciousness, leading to alienation from ourselves, the world, and God, and culminating in the absurdity of personal and societal decline.

THOMAS ON ORIGINAL JUSTICE

Sin is a negative reality. In other words, at least as Christian theology has classically understood sin, it has more to do with our *failure* to love than with our *commission* of specific acts. Of course, sin does have to do with committing sinful acts, but to understand what those acts are, what makes them sinful, and what they mean about us, it is necessary first to consider the way things should be. By sinning, we fall short of our purpose and the heart of our nature—to be the glory of God come into this world.[1]

---

1. This insight is essentially Augustinian. See Augustine, *On Free Choice of the Will*, Book II, 68–69.

Sinfulness is like a shadow. A shadow is a specific lack of the light. One will never understand a shadow simply by analyzing darkness. Shadows presuppose and depend on light. Human sinfulness, therefore, does have an intelligible nature, but only becomes understandable in dialectic with the life of wisdom and love that we are offered by God.[2] Sinfulness by itself has no such intelligible nature—it is a withdrawal from wisdom and love—but the contours of this withdrawal can be understood in relation to the light of that wisdom and love.

When Thomas Aquinas set out to analyze sin, therefore, he spoke first of the original righteous reality humans are intended to have in relationship with God. In Thomas' terms, this reality is called "original justice." He referred this state to the existence of Adam and Eve in the Garden of Eden before the Fall.[3]

Original justice indicates the right relation of human beings, as we are created, to God. It has three parts: right relation of our reason to God, the subsequent right relation of our lower powers (such as will and appetite) to our reason, and the consequent right relation of our body and soul.[4] Righteousness does not consist of being made by God, having a reason, having will and appetites, and being composed of body and soul. Righteousness consists in having those realities rightly ordered to each other. If the body is subject to the soul, if the soul itself is rightly ordered by having the appetites subject to the will and the will following the rule of reason, and if human reason continually submits to and learns from God who made it, then the entire human person will be a harmonious, just, reality.[5]

THE DISRUPTION OF THE WILL

As Aquinas understood it, Adam and Eve's sin did not only make them guilty before God. It also effected a radical change in their being. Just as justice consists in the right ordering of being, so the effects of sin cause disorder to replace that order.

---

2. See Lonergan, *Insight*, 214–31 and 244–69 on bias and 372–98 on the intelligible nature of being.

3. *ST* I-II 81.1–2.

4. *ST* I 95.1–2.

5. Cf. the connection in Plato's *Republic* of justice with harmony.

'Ihe center of sin's wound is the will.[6] Wills are made to tend toward the good—that is the natural and intrinsic function and nature of a will. But after the Fall, our wills no longer purely tend toward the good; we also love the darkness. We do not thereby cease to have a will. Our wills are damaged, not annulled in their being. But, just having a reason, will, appetites, etc., does not constitute righteousness. That we have become slaves to evil means that the will we have no longer measures up to the intrinsic requirements of its nature—loving the good, and the good alone.

Aquinas here follows Augustine's lead, for Augustine saw concupiscence as the root from which grows sin's foul flowers.[7] Concupiscence is disordered desire. It means to love that which we should not love, or to love that which we should love in the wrong way. For example, it is right to love music, but it is wrong to love a symphony more than one's family. It is wrong to love murder, but the human heart is capable of taking joy in this act. In these examples, our desire has gone awry, leaving us bereft of the righteousness we are designed to have.

But sin exactly involves a failure to love. It is not simple moral failure, for humans are not created simply as moral beings. We are made for a transcendent love relationship with God that leads to right relationship with others and with ourselves. Hence, even in the state of original justice, Adam and Eve lived in continual need and with the consistent experience of God's grace.[8] In that our fallen wills are corrupted by sin, the love that we should give to God we give to something else (often ourselves), and the rest of our loves reflect this fundamental disorder.

Because our righteousness consists of an ordered harmony of the different aspects of our being, the wounding of the will in the Fall devastates our entire being.[9] Our appetites become unmeasured, for the will no longer rightly regulates them by responsible choosing. Our physical nature no longer seamlessly serves our intellectual, moral, and appetitive nature, but is subject to breakdown and even becomes the source of disordered desires and irrational thoughts.[10]

6. *ST* I 81.1.

7. Augustine, *On Free Choice*, Book I, 6–7.

8. *ST* I 81.2.

9. For an extensive account of this devastation, see Snell, "Thomism and Noetic Sin, Transposed," 7–28.

10. One does not have to follow Freud's materialism to see the powerful role of our

Even our rational nature, itself, is damaged. One could understand this damage in several ways. One could mean that logic is different for fallen human beings than for those who were in the state of original justice. Thomas did not mean that. Logic is simply the science of the right relation of rational operations, and our rational operations—just as our wills—still exist in us. But the goal of our rational nature is to know the truth, meaning that our intellect, according to its own norms in the way it is created, tends toward and seeks the truth. But tending toward the truth is a type of desire, an intellectual *eros*. Because of the disruption of our will, and the consequent disruption of who we are as desiring beings, our reason sometimes still seeks, but often turns away from, the search for truth.[11]

This failure and disorder of reason indicates the deep rift opened between fallen human beings and their Creator. Thomas believed that God's nature is ultimately rational, the most rational of all. Just as God is *ipsum esse* (existence itself), he is also *ipsum intelligere* (understanding itself).[12] God is rational in a way that is beyond us, just as the light of the noonday sun exceeds the capacity of the eyes of a bat.[13] But the eyes of a bat are genuinely responsive to light, just as our natures should be intrinsically responsive to reason. God's being is unknowable to us because of the excess of its intelligibility, not because of a defect in its intelligibility. We will never know or understand the way that God does, even in heaven, for that would require becoming the essence of God.[14] But the kind of nature that we have is designed to find fulfillment in knowing the ultimate truth and goodness that is God himself.[15] That our reasons are no longer fit for that perfect union, due to the disruption of their pure tendency toward truth, indicates the way in which by losing

---

material being in the shaping of what we call our consciousness. See especially Freud, *Interpretation of Dreams*.

11. *ST* I-II 9.1. See Snell, "Thomism and Noetic Sin, Transposed," 14–17.

12. *ST* I 3.4, 16.5. For a treatment of exactly what Thomas means by these phrases and their relation to issues in modern, medieval, and ancient philosophy, see Lonergan, "Regis College Institute on the Method of Theology," 128–54. See also Brock, "On Whether Aquinas' 'Ipsum Esse' is 'Platonism,'" 269–303, on the differences between Aquinas' understanding and a purely Platonic one.

13. *ST* I 12.1.

14. *ST* I 12.7.

15. *ST* I 26.3.

our right relationship with God we have also lost the very substance of who we ourselves are.

Like ripples radiating out from a stone striking water, so the woundedness of our will throws our being ever more deeply into confusion. The highest relation a human being has to that which is above her is love.[16] Because of our choice against the wisdom of God, we have failed in that most essential love relation. The rightness of our being depends on sets of right relations, flowing from and culminating in right relationship with God. The disorder of our being, given our failure to love the good and seek the true, proceeds not just as God's judgment on us but as the reality of what it means to withdraw ourselves from the wisdom and love of God.

Perhaps the most pernicious aspect of this disorder consists in the way it is impossible for us to get ourselves out of our fallen condition. In one respect, we have become guilty before God and cannot atone for this offense on our own terms.[17] But even if God were to wipe our sinful guilt away, offering us a clean slate and a new chance, we still would not by that fact alone return to fellowship with him. For we have come to love the darkness (John 3:19). How well we understand the diabolical affirmation, "Better to reign in Hell than serve in Heaven."[18] Having lost the justice of our being in which we are rightly ordered in ourselves and toward God, we turn our loves to lesser things, loving the creature more than the Creator, who is blessed forever and ever (Romans 1:25).

CONSONANCE AND CONTRAST WITH
REFORMED DOCTRINE OF SIN

The understanding of Thomas that we have just presented is one that is subject to controversy.[19] This controversy has extended the length of 20th century Roman Catholicism. In many ways, aspects of it reflect the labors to reform Thomism by such pioneers as Henri de Lubac, Etienne Gilson, Karl Rahner, Bernard Lonergan, and Hans Urs von Balthazar.[20]

---

16. *ST* II-II 23.6 ad. 1.

17. This is the basic affirmation of Anselm in *Cur Deus Homo*.

18. John Milton, *Paradise Lost*, Book I.

19. See Kerr, *After Aquinas*.

20. We will simply point to the controversy raised by De Lubac's *Surnaturel*, published in 1946 and still untranslated in English. See Milbank, *The Suspended Middle*.

It is also a view that is strongly at variance with Reformed criticisms of Thomas' anthropology and soteriology.[21]

At the heart of this controversy is the relation between nature and grace. In the position we have staked out for Thomas above, created human nature exists permeated by grace. Such is, we maintain, clearly Thomas' own position.[22] But being created in grace is a strange idea.[23] We tend to differentiate nature and grace, whereby that which is by nature is not by grace.

As Thomism developed in the centuries after Thomas, it seemed necessary to many of his followers to separate nature clearly from grace in order to affirm both the effectiveness of God's creative act and the gratuity of salvation.[24] If human nature, in its very creation, is in need of grace, is it not a radically incomplete reality, something not worthy of being the crown of God's creation, because it does not a have a complete nature itself? And if a need for grace is somehow intrinsic to nature, is it not owed by God to the being he is creating? But God is in no one's debt, nor is God's creative work in any way ineffective.

But by affirming a "pure nature" distinct from grace, Thomas' followers seemed to be affirming a natural reality independent of God's supernatural nature. If nature is something that has no intrinsic connection to grace and need of it, then it seems autonomous. Grace would be able to add on to nature—build another story on the house—but created human nature itself would necessarily seem to be able to function and find the fulfillment of its being on its own terms.

Several Reformed theologians vociferously protested such an understanding of reality. Hermann Dooyeweerd, for instance, described Thomas Aquinas' nature-grace distinction as one of the two major competitors in Western thought with the biblical doctrine of creation and redemption.[25] And Dooyeweerd would be right, if Thomas actually had

21. See Snell, "Thomism and Noetic Sin, Transposed," for an examination of the Reformed criticism of Thomas' understanding of sin, nature, and grace.

22. ST I 95.1. See Lonergan, *Grace and Freedom*, 14–20, for the historical set-up of the problem.

23. In the *Summa* article referenced above that clearly states Thomas' position, he has to address no fewer than six objections. More would be developed in subsequent centuries.

24. For two contrasting views of this development, see Long, *Natura Pura*, and Cunningham, "Natura Pura," 243–54.

25. Dooyeweerd, *Twilight of Western Thought*, 40–44. The Greek philosophical model of matter and form is the other competitor he identifies.

taught the doctrine of a "pure,"—meaning autonomous—nature. For, there would then be no intrinsic role of the voice of God in defining his creation, but only an extrinsic one.

Reinhold Niebuhr, as well, especially criticized Thomas' understanding of fallen human nature. Niebuhr equated Thomas' "fallen human beings" with humanity understood in the terms of Greek philosophy, especially Aristotle. "[Fallen man] has a capacity for natural virtue which is subject to the limitations of man immersed in finiteness."[26] And if Thomas had taught that human nature could be complete and itself separated from relation with God, then Niebuhr would be right. Kant clearly showed that the demands of ethical living cannot be satisfied by knuckling-under to a heteronymous standard.[27] But if human nature is purely autonomous from God's supernatural nature, then it would be precisely heteronymous with respect to God's revelation and grace.

More than that, it would seem that human nature would need to be able to find its completion on its own terms. For, human nature on these terms exists autonomously, and it is not clear that the loss of grace would then necessarily impair human function and being. In fact, Thomas approved the Aristotelian notion that "nature fails in nothing necessary."[28] What is more necessary to human nature than achievement of its purpose and goal? A natural beatitude—happiness and completion—seems necessary to affirm, distinct from the supernatural beatitude of heaven. Thomas does so affirm.[29] But in doing so, does he not fall foul of Niebuhr's righteous critique?

Lonergan, though, is able to show that Thomas' doctrine can withstand this critique.[30] First, it is a mistake to understand the natural and the supernatural, or nature and grace, only in terms of non-contradiction. The natural and supernatural orders are not two complete realities existing parallel to each other. First, and preeminently, exists the being of God alone. Created being exists, and can only exist, by the act of God's eternal and uncreated being. A relation of dependence on God is intrin-

---

26. Niebuhr, *Nature and Destiny of Man*, 1:153n4.

27. Kant, *Religion within the Limits of Reason Alone*, 3–10.

28. *ST* I-II 5.5.

29. *ST* I-II 5.3.

30. See Lonergan, *Triune God: Systematics*, 653–55.

sic to created nature; in fact, this asymmetric relation of dependence constitutes what it means for created nature to exist.[31]

Second, because God creates wisely, he can bring about an intelligible order in what he creates. God therefore can establish an intelligible relation between nature and grace. This relation does not negate nature but rather indicates what nature actually is. Nature, to be itself and a really existing created reality, needs not absolute autonomy but relation to the divine. Such a relation exists both potentially and actually by the wise and omnipotent action of God.

Third, while nature fails in nothing necessary, the provision by which nature supplies its needs can be of different sorts. Perfect happiness and beatitude cannot be intrinsically available to created human nature apart from God, for perfect beatitude is natural for God alone.[32] But an imperfect beatitude could be available to created human nature on its own terms. One must recall, though, that because the relation of nature and grace is not perfectly described by mere non-contradiction, the terms of created nature include a reliance on and need for grace— even to achieve an imperfect beatitude, let alone the fulfillment of human being in the beatific vision of God.

Thomas offers a striking metaphor that illustrates this point.

> Just as nature does not fail man in necessaries, although it has not provided him with weapons and clothing, as it provided other animals, because it gave him reason and hands, with which he is able to get these things for himself; so neither did it fail man in things necessary, although it gave him not the wherewithal to attain Happiness: since this it could not do. But it did give him free-will, with which he can turn to God, that He may make him happy. "For what we do by means of our friends, is done, in a sense, by ourselves" (Ethic. iii, 3).[33]

While Thomas' emphasis on the importance of free will in turning to God may not satisfy his Reformed critics, at the least one can see that he envisions no human reality whose blessedness is separate from the gift of God.[34] And they should be glad to see his emphasis on the work of

---

31. See Burrell, "Analogy, Creation, and Theological Language."

32. *ST* I 6.3.

33. *ST* I-II 5.5 ad. 1.

34. See Goris, "Divine Foreknowledge, Providence, Predestination, and Human Freedom," 99–122; see also Stebbins, *Divine Initiative*, 142–82.

Christ, the friend of sinners, union with whom through the Holy Spirit makes us to be friends with God.[35]

Thomas did believe that a "certain participation of Happiness can be had in this life."[36] For, we do enjoy much of the goodness of God in this life, and the saved enjoy hope grounded on the sure promise of the fullness of that goodness in the world to come. This enjoyment is imperfect, however, in that we are subject to many evils and are doomed to die. Most of all, we lack the full communion with God of which perfect beatitude consists.

The evil Thomas especially pointed to here is the disordered state of our nature as a result of sin.[37] Our intellect no longer effectively and consistently seeks and finds truth. Our desires often are directed to destruction. And our bodies experience many evils that result from the disorder of our being. All of these result from the wound of sin, in which our wills turn away from and lose their original right relation to the good. The ultimate consequence of this disorder is the destruction of our being in death (Romans 6:23).

LONERGAN'S TRANSPOSITION FROM FACULTY PSYCHOLOGY

One of the difficulties with Thomas' approach, despite the depth of his insight, is his analysis of the human person in terms of a soul composed of separate faculties of intellect, will, and appetite. It is arguable that Thomas always has a unified human person in view. For instance, when he speaks of the will, he means the ability we have to make responsible choices; when he speaks of the intellect, he means the capability we have to seek out and find truth. But because he followed Aristotle in segregating these capacities into different aspects or powers of the soul, the unity of the human person becomes something that one must construct out of these quite differing components. And in the analysis of human cognition and action, it becomes possible to set one faculty, or power, against another. So the will becomes something that can be opposed with the intellect, and one can have arguments about which of them really has precedence.

---

35. See *ST* II-II 23.1 and III 26.1.

36. *ST* I-II 5.3.

37. Ibid.

These difficulties can be very difficult to overcome in the terms of a faculty psychology because none of the relevant faculties (intellect, will, appetite) are available for us directly to inspect them. We know them only by deduction from the way that human beings are able to interact with the world. We can understand propositions, so there must be some ability we have to understand; we choose one verbal formulation over another, so there must be some ability we have to make rational choices. And so forth. But the faculties themselves, and the habits whose presence can give them a settled disposition, are not directly available to us.

Lonergan believed that truly to follow Aquinas it would sometimes be necessary to go beyond him. As discussed in the last chapter, knowing a reality means to know the meanings that mediate its existence to us. Lonergan believed that both Aristotle and Thomas recognized this fundamental point of intellectual conversion, but he did not believe that the method they used to understand the human person fully took advantage of this insight.

Especially, Thomas proceeds with an understanding of the human person that depends only on an objective, extrinsic point of view. In other words, the study of the human person and the study of plants are carried out in precisely the same terms. Aristotle analyzed plants in terms of their souls: the nutritive ability that defines what it is to be alive for a plant. In a parallel way, he analyzed the human soul as having understanding and sensation that the plant does not.

This analysis is valid as far as it goes, but it does not take advantage of the fact that being a human studying human nature is different from being a human studying plants. Lonergan put it this way:

> A . . . source of neglect of the subject is the metaphysical [Thomist/ Aristotelian] account of the soul. As plants and animals, so men have souls. As in plants and animals, so in men the soul is the first act of an organic body . . . . The study of the soul, then, is totally objective. One and the same method is applied to study of plants, animals, and men. The results are completely universal. We have souls whether we are awake or asleep, saints or sinners, geniuses or imbeciles.[38]

Because the being of the universe is mediated to us through sets of meanings, it makes a difference to us whether we are studying a plant, for whom we have only external access to meaning, or whether we are

38. Lonergan, "The Subject," in *Second Collection*, 72.

studying a human, whose rational consciousness we both have and are. While the method of Thomas and Aristotle on this point attempts to be objective, it does not achieve this goal with respect to the world mediated by meaning. For being objective in the world mediated by meaning means to follow one's questions, wherever they go, adverting to all the sources of data and seeking insight into the data by every intelligent means.

No blame attaches to Thomas for this oversight; he used the best anthropology available at the time in the Western tradition and improved on it in several respects. But failing to utilize our privileged place as humans in studying humanity is forgetful of data that is available to us. Moreover, to make up for this lack, categories of understanding (for example, intellect, will, and soul) are supplied according to which manifest human experience can be organized.

Lonergan's intention was to study human subjectivity according to the operations of our consciousness.

> The study of the subject is quite different, for it is the study of oneself inasmuch as one is conscious. It prescinds from the soul, its essence, its potencies, its habit, for none of these are given in consciousness. It attends to operations and to their center and source, which is the self. It discerns the different levels of consciousness.[39]

Note that prescinding from something does not mean denying it. But Lonergan's intention was to analyze the human subject as she is conscious of and as herself. This consciousness is not one that comes prepackaged in separate faculties of intellect, appetite, and will. It proceeds from the factical subject (concretely existing, in Heidegger's terms, as Being-There).

In Lonergan's understanding, then, the exercise of intellect and will are not separate powers of the rational soul. Rather, the unified subject experiences the world (hopefully attentively), attempts to understand this experience (hopefully intelligently), and tries to discern which, if any, of her understandings actually is the case (hopefully reasonably). At the fully existential level, "consciousness becomes conscience," and she deliberates about how, then, she should live and what kind of person she should therefore be (hopefully responsibly). Each of these conscious op-

---

39. Ibid., 73.

erations is related to the others, and the later conscious operations bring the former into a broader horizon. For it is not one "I" that experiences the world and another "I" that understands it. It is just we, ourselves, as we try to live authentically in the world.

BIAS

Or, it is just we, ourselves, as we do not try to live authentically in the world. As Lonergan attempted to understand what it means for a unitary, factical, subject to bear the wound of sin, he did so under a number of different terms. By speaking of bias, inauthenticity, alienation, absurdity, lovelessness, and decline, Lonergan attempted to bring the essential insights of Aquinas and Augustine into a broader horizon and add to them the insights gained from studying the human subject within that horizon.

While it is not clear that any of these terms have pride of place in Lonergan's overall understanding of sin, one that has an especially fruitful application for the present discussion is bias. In his discussion of bias, Lonergan especially brings out the way that our failure to love manifests itself in our cognition. Bias has to do, in Lonergan's analysis, with a "scotosis."[40] Literally, scotosis indicates a blind spot, a loss of visual ability in a particular region of the visual field. Metaphorically, scotosis indicates an intellectual hardening in which certain insights are refused or suppressed.

Lonergan analyzed the effects of sin on our cognitive processes in terms of four main biases: individual, group, general, and dramatic.[41] Each of these biases indicates a flight from understanding. In other words, in the process of our experience of the world, we may not pay attention to certain aspects of reality. Likewise, our process of understanding may not admit certain questions as valid, or systematically may avoid certain answers to our questions. As we weigh the evidence and move toward knowledge, we may not consider all the relevant factors or give them the appropriate weight. And in our decision-making we

---

40. Lonergan, *Insight*, 215.

41. Ibid., 214, 244, 247, and 250. There is some difference in the explanation of bias between Lonergan's early and later writings. This chapter will speak mainly from the standpoint of his later writings, drawing on the foundational expression in his earlier treatment.

may not consider every relevant option on the same terms. Humans are finite, and each of these oversights can simply be the result of that finitude. But in many, many cases what is actually happening is an illegitimate refusal on our part to allow our conscious operations to follow their natural course.

Individual bias is perhaps the simplest of these flights from understanding to understand. It amounts to selfishness, or personal egoism.[42] For some reason, it is easy for us to overlook the advantages we have and take in the situations in which we live. For some reason, we tend not to see the reasonableness of insights that would call us to self-sacrifice. That reason is called sin. Individual bias, as an aspect of sin, indicates our ability and tendency to suppress the insights by which we would look not just to our personal good but also to the overall good.

Shadows exist as parasites of the light. Individual bias is not pursuit of evil, absolutely; rather it is pursuit of a limited good. For, our own benefit is a genuine good. There is nothing wrong with pursuing a limited good unless that pursuit compromises our commitment to the overall good. In individual bias, we privilege the limited perspective and disadvantage the pursuit of good that would not be of benefit for us. In so doing, we refuse to follow our own better inclinations; for we are made as beings who tend toward the good. By substituting our own limited good for that which is truly and simply good, we sacrifice something of our own being, for we must deny that part of us that is made to pursue and receive true blessedness—that which is most worthwhile.

Group bias is individual bias on a larger scale.[43] It indicates the ability of a group to form narratives that are narcissistic or that privilege its own members and commonly held understandings in an illegitimate way. Note, again, that it is not wrong for a group to form narratives by which it has a sense of identity. These commonly held stories and ideals are essential for groups. Nor is it wrong for a group to come to commonly held understandings. It would be impossible for each of us to operate in the world without receiving much of our common sense from our groups. Rightly done, this collaborative growth of insight forms the mesh of practical wisdom in which we are embedded. Nor is it wrong to have concern—even a special concern—for the members of one's own group.

42. Ibid., 244–47.
43. Ibid., 247–50.

But it is wrong when these narratives, understandings, and special concerns prevent us from interacting with others in a fair, open, and honest way. Just as personal egoism is the death-knell of legitimate self-love, so the ideologies and prejudices of group bias pervert the legitimate function of community. For the purpose of commonly held understandings is to allow us to live more intelligently and reasonably in the world. The narratives of our group are supposed to enable us to know our identities as authentic human beings. And the special bonds of friendship and fraternity are supposed to be the means by which we live out truth and love together. In group bias, we listen to our group's point of view in a way that keeps us from giving other points of view a fair hearing. We make our story to be the master story, the story by which other groups should be judged; in so doing we fail to hear and know those whom we meet. And we bind ourselves to the validity of our fellows in a way that violates the validity of those with whom we do not share that bond.

Group bias is a more pernicious foe than individual bias, though any form of bias indicates a deep sickness of the human person. Most groups include in their common wisdom admonitions against personal egoism. But who protects a group from the voice of the group itself? The way that we make most of our judgments indicates our enmeshment in a group. Because it has such potential to go unchecked, group bias has more potential than individual bias to lead to a cycle of decline in which a group's common wisdom and values over time become more and more absurd.[44]

Whereas both individual and group bias indicate flights from understanding that have to do with contemporaneous subjects, general bias indicates a particular scotosis active across time.[45] In particular, it indicates the tyranny of the present over a long-term point of view. Because we live in the present, and can only do so, we can tend to privilege those understandings and values that seem to us of immediate practicality.

Again, pursuing practicality is not wrong. But in many cases the most intelligent course may involve steps whose utility will only appear over the long-term. In "pursuing practicality," we often mean disparaging those ideas whose practicality is apparent only over centuries in favor of that which we hope will lead to short-term gain.

---

44. Ibid., 249–50.

45. Ibid., 250–51. See also Flanagan, *Quest for Self-Knowledge*, 84–85.

Understanding general bias requires differentiating between two different ways of trying to understand the world. One way—the way our common sense normally directs us toward—attempts to understand the world as it relates to us. Another way—which one could call theoretical—attempts to understand the sets of relations that exist in the world, irrespective of their connection to us. Because we live in the present, our common sense understandings tend to privilege what is immediately useful. Theoretical understandings, on the other hand, express insights that may or may not be of utility at all; they do not have concern for how we are practically to live but rather for what the right relations of things are to other things in this world.

No human being could make it through an hour without some application of common sense. The problem comes when common sense—that immediately present and always active form of understanding—limits all valid forms of inquiry to its own point of view dominated by immediate practicality. But theoretical insights may provide the eventual solution to the problems common sense faces. Even in terms of practicality, then, we are shortsighted in our thinking when we limit our thinking to what we can take home and use today. And in terms of the pursuit of truth—the true expression of who we are as questioning beings—the tyranny of the present in general bias radically limits the questions we are willing to ask and the answers we are willing to pursue.

Group bias leads to decline, but it does so in ways that sow the seeds of its own reversal.[46] Group bias operates, by and large, in terms of common sense. It is *our* group, *my* family, *our* story and enemy that group bias concerns; the world as related to us and me. Because it fails to pursue the relevant questions in a fair way, it will over time lead to a failure to find effective answers to these questions. As the group narrative, and its results, become more and more absurd, it more and more fails to satisfy the demands of the form of intelligence that it reflects: common sense. And because common sense seeks out practicality, the group's existence in the world becomes more and more impractical. In the decline of its society, then, the group gradually looses the ability to perpetuate its distorted narrative.

General bias, on the other hand, can lead to decline on a much longer and larger scale.[47] Group bias can be weighed and found wanting

46. Lonergan, *Insight*, 249–50.
47. Ibid., 251–67.

in the terms of common sense, the form of intelligence from which it springs. But general bias can only be adequately judged from a theoretical viewpoint, a viewpoint that expressly denies the privilege of short-term practicality. However, it is precisely this viewpoint that general bias has ruled out of court.

Consider, for example, the function of an intellectual "think-tank," or policy institute. Policy institutes can be powerful instruments for the promotion of understanding. However, they can also be instruments of propaganda and fronts for special interest groups. What is the difference between the two? Which type of group is more likely to receive funding? To the extent that short-term practicality rules, the latter type of group will likely be privileged. This mistake will likely be repeated in the chambers of the policy makers that the think-tanks exist to influence, for both groups respond to the same tyranny of the present. And when general bias becomes part of the bias of a group, an especially destructive dynamic comes into existence.[48] For then the narrative and resources of the group become directed to a more and more absurd pursuit of short-term gain in contrast to the overall pursuit of truth.

ALIENATION

In all of these cases, we lose who we really are. The heart of our being, as we are intended to be, does not consist in a flight from understanding. But because our loves have become distorted, we no longer rightly pursue the truth. Bias reflects a lack of love in that in each instance we fail to treat another person or another viewpoint in the way that we would wish to be treated ourselves and in the way we would wish our viewpoints to be considered. We have failed to love the truth and so seek it at cost. Sin is not just moral failing, but a "radical dimension of lovelessness."[49] We have come to love the true and the good only from a limited point of view, which is a failure to love truth and goodness as they really are.

And so we become strangers to each other and strangers to ourselves. Individual, group, and general bias indicate the alienation we experience from the reality and value of the world of being with which we relate. But the deepest bias can also indicate the alienation we experience in terms of who we are.

48. Ibid. See also Flanagan, *Quest for Self-Knowledge*, 86–89.
49. Lonergan, *Method*, 242–43.

Lonergan's examination of this bias varies from his earlier work to his later work. In his earlier work, he speaks of dramatic bias.[50] In his later work, he deals with the same subject from a different viewpoint in terms of the bias of the unconscious motivations, the root of radical sin within us.[51] In either case, he is explaining the way we have become strangers to ourselves because we have become strangers to the light.

Dramatic bias refers to the way that we become untrue to ourselves because we appraise the performance of our lives and find it wanting.[52] Lonergan here especially refers to the function of the "censor" that Freud explains in his psychodynamic theories. The operation of our neural processes and the progress of our growth and development contain aspects that we are unwilling or unable to face in fully conscious life. And so we repress the images that would lead to the insights we do not want to have, allowing them entry into consciousness in the distorted world of dreaming, if at all.

Note, again, that Lonergan (as would Freud) understands the defense mechanisms of our consciousness often to operate in a helpful and necessary way. The exigencies of growing beings who must maintain psychic unity require the existence and operation of psychic censorship. But our defense mechanisms do not always operate in this sanguine way. Even without the development of clinical neuroses, we often turn away from the conduct and meaning of our lives in shame. We thereby become distorted in our being as ourselves.

In his later work, Lonergan linked this bias to the sets of images and feelings that live in "the twilight of consciousness."[53] Feelings communicate value to us, and images (especially as symbols) are instrumental in mediating meaning. In the bias of the unconscious motivation, Lonergan points to the way that because our feelings have become distorted (most centrally in the failure to love), we are limited in the way we receive the stream of insights and feelings that mediate the being and value of the world. Because we cannot face up to aspects of who we are—because we know that we do not follow the better lights of our own being—we become lost to ourselves, and this loss of self leads us to a radically compromised relation with the world.

50. Lonergan, *Insight*, 214–31.

51. Lonergan, "Moral Theology and the Human Sciences," 309.

52. Lonergan, *Insight*, 214–15.

53. Lonergan, *Method*, 35n5 and 35n6.

Phenomenologically considered, it is the root of radical sin within us.[54] We choose to love the darkness, because our deeds are evil (John 3:19). Because we cannot just reach into our hearts and change our feelings, this disorder of our unconscious motivation indicates a situation of moral impotence. Lonergan would encourage pursuit of wholeness through different methods of self-appropriation.[55] But because we are alienated from ourselves we have become unable to a great extent to uncover the roots of inauthenticity within us. In order for our being as ourselves to be right-being, something truly radical will have to change.

---

54. Ibid., 242–43, 364.
55. Ibid., 35n5 and 35n6.

5

The Graciousness of Being-There

Moral and Religious Conversion

Just as knowing and loving, and their disorder by sin, are best under-stood phenomenologically, so too ought grace be approached. God reworks human loves, and thus horizons, values, and identities, in ways accessible and understandable to the methods of self-appropriation. These concrete reorderings of love occur in moral and religious conver-sions, found in Augustine's *Confessions* and systematized in Lonergan's *Method in Theology*. These reorderings allow for the formation of au-thentic human subjects, in keeping with certain structural traits of the person identified by Heidegger and Taylor, most particularly in the domain of value and the affective. The subject experiences a change in horizon of expectation whereby he or she loves differently from before, based on the gift of God's love. Within this enlarged and transformed horizon the subject pursues authentic relation to values and being, a self-giving that is natural for rightly ordered love.

GRACE RECONSIDERED

As the foregoing analysis of sinfulness abundantly demonstrates, without the work of redemption and grace the human condition is dark indeed. But just as the account of sin becomes more real and better understood when considered phenomenologically, so also we better see the reality of God's transforming our lives when we proceed from an analysis of the phenomenon of human living. This type of analysis does not do away with the traditional metaphysical accounts of human being and action; rather it grounds them and shows their depth and power.

Bernard Lonergan's theological viewpoint connected with grace is undeniably grounded in the Western theological tradition of Augustine and Aquinas. However, in Lonergan's later theological development, he turns to the work of modern developmental psychologists in order to appropriate those insights. In particular, Lonergan turned to Jean Piaget's corpus and the later works of Abraham Maslow for their analyses of experienced and understood human living. Because Lonergan considered all genuine works of the human spirit to have a kind of permanent validity, this turn does not mean he left behind the theology of Augustine and Aquinas. It rather shows the vigor of those understandings that their validity comes to be appreciated in a more powerful way when approached in more modern terms.

To see the force of this transposition, it will be helpful briefly to examine aspects of Lonergan's grace theology in its earlier (Thomist) terms. These insights from his early writings give an account of God's work in saving us that Lonergan explicitly indicates he never left behind.[1] With that account in mind, we can better appreciate the way Lonergan brings those insights within the horizon of contemporary understandings of human growth and transformation.

SANCTIFYING GRACE

A great deal of Lonergan's early theological work revolved around the question of what it means that God works to change us by saving us. Building on the work of Thomas Aquinas (who was himself strongly Augustinian in this regard), Lonergan especially analyzed the psychological aspects of grace. His conviction, which he argued as being present in Aquinas, was that the work of saving grace transforms our conscious operations and is present to us in a way that is knowable.[2] He also was convinced that by saving us, God initiates in us a life that is supernatural.[3]

Thomas understood sanctifying grace as connected to the habits of faith, hope, and charity. The Mission of the Spirit and the Mission of the Word create in us a new life in which we trust God, believe the truth about him, and come to see the world as coming from and ordered

---

1. Lonergan, *Method*, 107n5.
2. Lonergan, *Grace and Freedom*, 54–55.
3. Stebbins, *Divine Initiative*, 35.

to him. On the basis of this faith, we love the God that we have come to know. This love, a true friendship with God, renews and reorders us within. Our choices and desires come to have a new basis because we have been changed by the gift of God's love. Finally, we come to live a life motivated by the hope of heaven. In other words, because we know God and trust him, and because we have been changed within by his love, we come to live a life based on his promises. Because we trust these promises—resurrection and the life of heaven—we habitually come to live in a way that makes sense in eternal perspective, a life that is ordered to eternal life.[4]

Note that in all of these transformations, while the basis of the change involves our underlying nature, the result of the change is a revolution in how we think and live. Habits (such as faith, hope, and charity) become second nature to us, modifying the way that we exist in the world. Habits are not known directly but are deduced from the regular way in which we act. In the acts, though, we become conscious of the changes that have been made in our nature. We become conscious of God's action in us because of the renovation in what we believe, love, and commit ourselves to.

What we become conscious of is nothing less than the beginning in us of eternal life.[5] In faith, we assent to divine truth and to the trustworthiness of God. In hope, we receive certainty that God will save us, bringing us to eternal life through knowing him. In charity, we receive friendship with God. All of these realities point to a life that is still to come but also received in a real way now. For faith and hope point to the complete knowledge and blessedness of heaven, and charity brings about the central aspect of that life in us now.

All of these actions are beyond the innate capacity of human nature. An effect must be proportionate to its cause. But the effects of salvation (knowing God, receiving eternal blessedness, being the friend of God) are beyond the ability of human beings to produce.[6] In fact, they are proportionate only to the nature of God, for only God fully knows God, and only God is able to produce and secure an infinite happiness. Friendship,

---

4. See, for example, Thomas' definition of faith in *ST* II-II 4.1.

5. Ibid.

6. *ST* I-II 109.5.

likewise, requires a measure of equality between the friends.[7] But only God is equal to God.

Therefore, in faith, hope, and charity we are receiving a new life. Because of the gift of God to us, we are able to receive a mode of life that is supernatural. In other words, what is natural for God (knowing divine truth, having eternal blessedness, being complete love) becomes in some way natural for us because we have received the gift of God's life. We receive this life as created beings: salvation means sharing in God's life by gift, not becoming God in our nature. Yet the gift of God's life does radically transform us by giving us new principles of our being.[8] Instead of being able only to love, hope, and know in human terms, we are given the ability to live out these conscious operations in a way that befits receiving the life of God.

By receiving this gift we fulfill the meaning of our created nature by going beyond it. As humans, the meaningful nature of our existence in the world requires from us participation in God's grace. As we argued in Chapter Four, natural human existence—human life as created—is saturated with grace. All of our natural capacities (wisdom, art, prudence, justice, etc.) are given to us as created beings and meant to be lived out in concert with communion with God. Yet the grace of salvation gives us something new. In this new way of being, we find the fulfillment of our natural capacities and desires, and much more. For, we receive a life in which communion with God has no end.

RELIGIOUS CONVERSION

When Lonergan attempts to understand sanctifying grace, appropriated in phenomenological terms, he explains it in terms of "religious conversion." He states that religious conversion is only notionally distinct from sanctifying grace.[9] That is, "religious conversion" and "sanctifying grace" refer to the same realities as explained under two different thought frameworks.

By "religious conversion," again, Lonergan does not necessarily mean changing one's religion. He refers to an inner work of God in which the principles of one's life are radically changed. This inner work

7. See *ST* II-II 23.1, adapting and augmenting Aristotle's discussion of friendship from the *Nicomachean Ethics*.

8. *ST* I-II 62.

9. Lonergan, *Method*, 107.

may or may not be understood by the person who receives it in religious terms.

For example, a radical Marxist who receives the work of God may not necessarily go on to become a Christian. Lonergan's theology is quite inclusivist at this point, pointing to the way that any genuine human appropriation of meaning depends on God's grace.[10] But, at the least, that person's way of being a Marxist will be changed. Love will be in play in way it was not before. The motivations of her heart will more and more tend to move toward what is genuinely of utmost concern, for realizing it or not she will have received an orientation toward the ultimate value of God.

Religious conversion refers to the inner work of God in which one's horizon of expectation is changed to love what one did not love before.[11] It transposes what Thomas explained as the invisible mission of the Holy Spirit into phenomenological terms. This inner transformation will be received in terms of an external tradition, for example Roman Catholic Christianity or Maoist Marxism. The outer word of tradition is not a mere husk, for the mission of the Spirit coordinates with and undergirds the Mission of the Word. But the work of religious conversion itself concerns the inner word of the heart that gives the outer tradition its validity and meaning.

GROWTH AS METAPHOR FOR ETERNITY

One of the striking aspects of both Thomas and Augustine's thought is their ability to use motion as a metaphor for eternity. Neither theologian believed that eternity changes. That which is eternal simply is; it never becomes. Yet to understand the fullness of this reality they both sometimes turned to images of motion.

The Trinity, for example, God's eternal being Three-in-One, is an eternal reality. Yet central to both Augustine and Thomas' understanding of the Trinity are highly dynamic images. Both find the highest analogy for the Trinity in the human mind, not as an inert substance, but as it is in motion, knowing and loving. Eternity simply goes beyond our temporal pairing of static versus dynamic realities. It is the source and ground of all that is.

10. Ibid., 118–19.
11. I thank Fred Lawrence for this phrase.

In religious conversion, or sanctifying grace, eternal life has begun to exist us. To understand the character of this life, grounded in the phenomenology of human existence, Lonergan turns to the work of developmental psychology. In growth—positive development—Lonergan sees a moving image that helps us understand the eternal character of the life that has come to be given to us.

Abraham Maslow, in his later psychology, worked out a striking understanding of what he termed growth needs and growth motivation. In Maslow's analysis, most traditional psychology centers on treating deficiencies in human living and being. That is, instead of studying mental health, psychology had studied mental disease, and health was being treated simply as the absence of disease.[12]

What Maslow pointed out is that growth actually has a distinct character of its own. Whereas some aspects of mental health do involve removing deficiencies, the deficiencies themselves are only rightly understood when compared with the character of right human development. And that right human development includes dynamics of change that are quite different from what is involved in curing deficiency.

For example, when a human deficiency such as hunger is cured—filled in—we cease to think about it. Solving the deficiency ends the issue, until another deficiency occurs. But when people grow, they tend to want to grow more. Rather than bringing the issue to a close, genuine growth leads to motivation toward more growth along the same lines or even branching out into other areas.[13]

A person who learns to play the violin, for example, does not usually reach proficiency with the instrument and then never pick up the violin again. He plays. He performs. He seeks out new types and avenues of music. The more mastery is gained, the more creativity is expressed in the playing. And if that person would stop being motivated this way, it is likely that the growth he formerly experienced is slowing or ceasing. But it is at least as likely that someone who has come to this point would have in front of him a lifetime of exploration in music.

One of the key discoveries Maslow set forth in his later work is that humans need growth to be healthy. And the different growth needs, as opposed to the deficiency needs, are non-hierarchical.[14] Whereas the

12. See Maslow, *Toward a Psychology of Being*, 21–43.

13. Ibid., 30–31.

14. Ibid., 97–98.

developmental needs explored by Maslow's earlier work express a strict ordering (one needs to have avoided starvation before one worries about the security of one's job), growth needs occur in a more spontaneous way. They are ordered with respect to their relative importance to our growth, but one does not have to work her way up the pyramid to experience the higher levels.

The highest level of growth need Maslow identified is what he labeled "self-transcendence." In his terms, it means living for a meaning that is greater than oneself. Self-transcendence differs from Maslow's earlier identification of self-actualization as the top of human needs. Self-actualization has to do with maximizing one's human capacities. In a way, it is a deficiency motivation, for in self-actualization one is doing away with the limited nature of one's self-expression. While extremely positive, self-actualization does not inherently lead to something beyond itself. It is the top of the pyramid, and here the blessed few would remain. But self-transcendence has to do with spiritual awakening and liberation from egocentricity. It explicitly is ordered to something beyond, something the individual person seeks, whose attainment is never complete. And as a growth motivation, as even partial success is achieved, the person is motivated to deeper authenticity and further self-transcendence.

HUMAN SKILLS AND DEVELOPMENT

Maslow provides a powerful paradigm of the dynamics of growth that Lonergan will transpose to explain the existence and character of supernatural life. To describe, however, the nature of the human person who is experiencing this growth, Lonergan used the findings of Jean Piaget. In the dynamics of adaptation and the development of skills, Piaget offers conceptual tools Lonergan will use to understand the habits of sanctifying grace.

The theologians of the Middle Ages, Aquinas included, worked within the logical framework provided by Aristotle's *Organon*. So powerful and complete was this work that while there were many struggles to understand, interpret, and extend different aspects of it, there was no basic and essential progress in logic until the development of modern mathematics. The classical logical paradigms gave the basic shape and character to the forms of thought expressed in Ancient and Medieval theology and philosophy.

When Aristotle found a coordinated set of actions, therefore, he looked for some common factor that would coordinate them all. For example, when the same person is honest at playing cards, in filing her taxes, and in keeping a promise made to a friend, Aristotle looked for some extra coordinating factor to make sense of this common intelligibility. In specific, he deduced habits, such as justice, that were conceived as behind-the-scenes operators that produced the coordinated actions. This deduction was necessary, given the logical framework Aristotle had been able to work out. The actions are each viewed as isolated instances, and if no underlying coordinating factor is found then no common intelligibility could be found.[15]

The development of group theory in the 1800s, a key aspect of modern mathematics, constituted a major advance in logic. Group theory develops and utilizes logical techniques to treat a group as an object. So, instead of having to find an external factor that accounts for coordinated action in a group, group theorists look to the inherent constitution of the group itself.

Piaget used group theory to understand the way the human consciousness develops.[16] Instead of looking for a behind-the-scenes operator, such as a habit, to account for coordinated aspects of growth and development, Piaget looked for dynamics of growth and development that are inherent in the structure of conscious itself. His discoveries about these structures form the basis of his theory of adaptation.

"Adaptation" is the word Piaget used in his overarching explanation of growth. Adaptation consists of twin complementary processes of assimilation and accommodation. When biological entities encounter objects or situations in the world, they attempt to integrate—assimilate—these objects or situations within existing structures of consciousness. Most types of growth consist of assimilation. That is, in most cases, we extend or enrich the current frameworks we have to account for new stimuli. However, in some cases, the existing framework that we have must be changed to account for new situations and data. In that case, we accommodate the new (or newly understood) reality by modifying our existing way of thinking and acting to fit the new situation.[17]

---

15. Aristotle, *Nicomachean Ethics*, 2.1, and Aquinas, *ST* I-II 49.

16. Piaget, "Intellectual Operations and Their Developments," 352–53.

17. Bringuier, *Conversations with Jean Piaget*, 42–43.

For example, consider the visit my (Steven Cone's) 19-month-old daughter recently made to the Shedd Aquarium in Chicago. One of the exhibits we saw was a large group of penguins. They stood up on the ledge over the water or swam with powerful strokes through the pool next to the glass. My daughter excitedly exclaimed, "Rabbit!" She loves animals, and her favorite ones now are rabbits; she also loves horses, dogs, cats, birds, fish, and squirrels. In naming the penguins as rabbits, she attempted to understand (assimilate) the penguins according to the thought framework she already had. And, I must admit that the smooth feathers of the penguins looked something like fur, and the powerful strokes they used to swim through the water resembled the ability of a rabbit to jump over the fields.

In response to her exclamation, I tried to explain that penguins are birds that swim in the water, not rabbits. When she is able to understand that, she will have made an important accommodation. In other words, she will have adjusted her thought processes to be able to account for a wider range of data in more creative ways than she had previously been able to attain.

In a way, every act of assimilation involves accommodation. The existing framework must always be applied to the new situation, and this application is not automatic. We adjust. But some situations (or sets of situations) call one to a more noticeable or dramatic accommodation. And even the most dramatic accommodations do not completely leave behind the old framework. Some of the forms of meaning are retained. Hence adaptation consists of a rich interplay of the subject's ability to live ever more fully in the world according to different dynamics of growth.

Many of Piaget's central insights pertained to the way that subjects seek what he called "equalibration."[18] Equalibraton indicates the inherent tendency of subjects to self-regulate by following the process of adaptation. Being an intelligent being in a changing world means undergoing dynamics of change. Rather than being biased to keep the level of growth that we have, we always are drawn to find new ways of understanding and living in a world we cannot master completely.

A major question Piaget pursued along these lines is whether the growth of the subject is more governed by the relations already present to it or by the dynamics of growth present within it. His research led him to affirm that although the sets of relations one already has and

18. Ibid., 43–45.

knows are important, the creative and formative processes of the human mind play the governing role.[19] Piaget called these growth dynamics, "transformations," and they play an essential role in the inherent growth motivation of the human subject.

Piaget termed the result of these transformations, "skills." Skills are the organization of intelligence as the result of growth. By possessing a skill, we are able to exist in the world in a more deeply intelligent way.

For example, children as young as two can learn to count. Understanding the numbers that go with given groups of objects and how to tick off fingers from one to ten is an organization of intelligence that the child did not have (and barring exceptional cases could not develop) a year earlier. In this case, the child has not just added a tool to her mental toolbox; rather, she has become a numbered person who is able to interact with her world in a more deeply intelligent way.

This same child, however, will not be able to think of numbers abstractly until around the age of seven. While around the age of two she has developed the skill (come to exist in the world according to an understanding) of numbers, these numbers are tied completely to concrete objects in her world. How many carrots? How many toes? But as an older child she can come to do mental mathematics in which numbers have an existence that it not limited by her sensory-motor skills. She will come to be able to understand the world in a broader way, in which mental activity has a significance that is not completely limited to what she can see, touch, hear, smell, or move through.

By privileging transformation, Piaget pointed to the way that the dynamics of growth present to this child, not the mere repetition of situations, govern the way she comes to exist in the world. No amount of teaching and repetition can allow a three year old to do mental mathematics. But the development of her behavior according to new patterns and insights will someday move that child to understand the same, given, situations in a dramatically new way. Her being in the world will be transformed based on a newly achieved organization of her intelligence.

Here is one place where the importance of group theory can be seen in Piaget. The different classifications of group theory help Piaget know what kinds of transformations to look for and what characteristics they might have. By finding the logic of these transformations, he is therefore able to supersede the earlier psychology of habit. In the

19. Ibid. 98–99.

conceptualization of habit, habit and the subject's nature are always at a conceptual remove from the actions he undertakes on objects. Because Piaget is capable of treating the coordinated sets of actions undertaken by a subject as one object (a group), he is able to see the new sets of relations themselves as the enactment of the subject's living intelligently in the world. Because the skills resulting from transformations are not passive things but themselves always point to new dimensions of needed growth, the inherent logic by which the human subject exists is one that leads toward growth.

MASLOW AND PEAK EXPERIENCE

The new dimensions allowed by developments of growth turn out to have surprising underpinnings and effects. In "peak experience," a second aspect of Maslow's later psychology, Lonergan finds a powerful analogy for the effects of love elevating our being in eternal life. Especially as applied to love, the analysis of peak experience provides a powerful way to understand the beginning of eternal life here.

As we mentioned above, Maslow in his earlier psychology expected self-actualization to complete the process of human growth and development. Yet as he surveyed many of his subjects, he came to believe that self-actualization only occurred in a small minority of cases. Because the fulfillment of this type of need is hierarchical, very few individuals were able to work through all the requisite stages. But in his interviews, including some with concentration camp survivors, Maslow came to believe that many people who had not achieved self-actualization would often, at least temporarily, live in a self-actualized way.[20]

Maslow came to believe that certain experiences can affect us in a way that allows us, at least temporarily, to live beyond the level of need-fulfillment that we have achieved. In particular, he looked to what he termed peak experiences as powerful dynamics of growth. In his estimation, they allow those who had no right to expect self-actualization to live in some respects as self-actualized people.[21]

The most common, though not the only, peak experience is falling in love. Peak experience can also be connected to the individual's feel-

---

20. Maslow, *Psychology of Being*, 71–131; and Maslow, *Religions, Values and Peak Experiences*, 91–102.

21. Maslow, *Psychology of Being*, 97.

ing of realizing or knowing an ultimate truth. The most powerful peak experiences include, in Maslow's terms:

> Feelings of limitless horizons opening up to the vision, the feeling of being. Simultaneously more powerful and also more helpless than one ever was before, the feeling of great ecstasy and wonder and awe, the loss of placing in time and space.[22]

These peak experiences are sung by our great lyricists, enshrined in epochal poetry, and humbly come before in true religion.

However, the maximal peak experiences are not the only kind. In fact, many people have peak experiences without ever realizing that they are doing so.[23] Peak experience involves a feeling of completion, of catharsis, of peace. It can be occasioned by a moving work of art, by the glory of nature, an inspiring personal example, or by falling in love. Whether the experience is recognized as something special or not, in peak experience the subject has become more complete.

Peak experience relates in a powerful way to Maslow's development of theories of growth motivation. Peak experience provides a mechanism by which the hierarchical nature of deficiency motivation can be overturned. Because we are drawn to self-transcendence, and thereby to a more spiritual reality, we become more open to living in a way that expresses wholeness of heart and mind. As we encounter realities that move us, change us, the way that we live (and are able to live) becomes transformed.

RELIGIOUS CONVERSION AND THE HORIZON OF GROWTH

Lonergan uses the aspects of human development that Piaget and Maslow present to explain the way that God changes us by his love. There are obvious difficulties with this approach. Anytime that created reality is used to explain the work of the Creator, it will fall short. This difficulty is built into any use of analogy, though; analogies always use the realities we know to explain what we do not know. The particular difficulty here is that exactly what Lonergan is trying to explain pertains to the difference between natural and supernatural life. It will therefore be of utmost importance to keep in mind the limited (but still powerful) nature of these analogies and not to understand them as a

22. Maslow, *Motivation and Personality*, 164.
23. See Maslow, *Psychology of Being*, 105.

"Great-Chain-of-Being," in which natural and supernatural life are not fundamentally different from each other. However, given that knowing God is the destiny of humans as created, even though the attainment of that goal is beyond our natural powers it is the fulfillment of who we are as created beings (and thereby of our natural capacities and needs). The elevation provided by grace will therefore have some commonality with the growth and healing of our natural being, for it is the human person in his very being that is both elevated and healed.

Most fundamentally, Maslow shows that humans are ordered to self-transcendence. When we are most fully being ourselves, we seek, know, and love the other. This fulfillment points to our nature as spiritual, both the core of who we are and our utmost fulfillment. And the points at which we grow in self-transcendence lead us to seek further fulfillment of our spiritual being.

But our ultimate self-transcendence is in love. In Lonergan's understanding, religious conversion is God's love given to us in a way that changes us. We are set in a horizon in which we are ordered to a self-transcendence that is radical and ultimate, for God is greater than and beyond this world. As we are authentic to this move of God's grace, we become ordered to his transcendent mystery in an unconditional way. We cannot grasp yet the one who calls us, but we know that we can never be the same.

Piaget's great insight was to understand and explain the nature of the transformations by which we achieve growth. As we grow, the dynamics of growth operative within us both empower us to live more fully in this world and draw us further on in intelligent adaptation. The skills we develop as a result of these transformations are not add-ons to who we are, nor are they behind-the-scenes operators. They are we, ourselves, as we live more deeply and more intelligently in the world.

But in religious conversion, God's love becomes the principle of our being. The transformations that become possible for us and that we are called to are those empowered by the radical presence of love. The way our being develops to live more fully in the world—our skills—become those of a person whose ultimate basis is love.

This love allows us to live in a way that we ordinarily would not be able to live. At the heart of Maslow's discussion of peak experience is this question: "How do seemingly ordinary people come to live in extraordinary ways?" Lonergan's analysis is two-fold. First, the "ordinary human person" is one whose destiny is full communion with the Godhead in a community of wisdom and love. Second, the gift of God's love is the ultimate experience that enables us to live out this destiny.[24]

The gift of God's love in religious conversion, though, is not a transient experience leading to a passing ability to self-transcend. Rather it a fundamental and permanent transformation of the human person by the Creator. While Maslow spoke of peak experience, perhaps in Lonergan's terms it would be better to speak of a dynamic peak state.[25] For as changed beings situated in the world, our very being becomes Being-in-Love.

In the work of developmental psychology, then, Lonergan finds a powerful analog to help explain life in the Spirit of God. Just as Augustine and Aquinas turned to the active nature of the human mind to explain the Trinitarian relations, so also Lonergan turns to the active transformation of the human spirit to explain the way that we receive the life of the Triune God. In religious conversion—the new life of love based on the gift of God—Lonergan shows the shape of a life that begins in us now and that will never end.

FEELINGS AS SKILLS OF THE KINGDOM

While the skills that Piaget analyzed often are taken purely in terms of intellectual development, he intended them to be applicable to any aspect of human behavior. This distinction is important in that Lonergan uses "skills" to transpose the earlier theology of "habit." The habits associated with sanctifying grace do include a transformed basis of intellectual operation in the habit of faith. But their foundation is the transformation of the human will in charity.

Lonergan did not differentiate sharply between two faculties of the human subject, intelligence and will, as Thomas did. Instead, Lonergan spoke of the related and recurrent operations of the unified human subject. When we ask and answer questions of fact, questions of possibility and actuality, the operations of our consciousness aim for intelligence and reasonableness. But when we live more fully in the world by making choices, our "consciousness becomes conscience."[26] We operate in

---

24. See Lonergan's discussion of "faith" in *Method*, 115–18.

25. Ibid., 107.

26. Ibid., 268.

regard to questions of responsibility and value. These operations are related because we enter into moral deliberation about the real situations we judge ourselves to be in and on the basis of how we understand our world. They are recurrent because questions of fact lead to questions of value, and our values form the basis of our search for truth in the world.

Lonergan defined "feelings" as intentional responses to value.[27] Here, Lonergan is drawing on the work of Max Scheler and Dietrich von Hildebrand, using language drawn from the phenomenological tradition. By "intentional," Lonergan means that feelings are directed toward and occasioned by particular realities. He does not mean that we do feelings "on purpose." In fact, feelings cannot be generated by us at will but must spontaneously occur. They are responses, for they occur in relation to the reality that we encounter and are occasioned by it. And they respond to value, for they mediate not the being but the good or evil of the occasioning reality as appropriated by us.

To take an example, consider a friend walking into a hospital room occupied by two parents and their sick child. As analyzed by Scheler, the two parents share a deep common bond of feeling: suffering and concern over their child. In a different but powerful way, the friend will come to share the parents' grief. Just as the intellectual meanings of "friend," "parent," "sick," and "child" mediate the being of this situation through concepts, so the shared pathos mediates the value of the situation through feelings.[28]

Von Hildebrand's work draws out the way that transformed feelings are the basis of how we are changed by God's gift of love.[29] Feelings have to do with motivation. When that which truly is worthwhile motivates us, and when we are motivated in proportion to how important something objectively is, then our moral being is in line with the objective good. When it is not, our moral being is distorted.

Von Hildebrand's point is basically Augustinian. According to Augustine, the gift of God's love is necessary for us to be moral beings because what we truly need to be moral is a good will.[30] A good will especially has to do with the way that we love, the transformation of our desire. Von Hildebrand draws out the richness of this Augustinian

27. Ibid., 30–34.

28. See Frings, *Max Scheler*, 56–66.

29. Von Hildebrand, *Christian Ethics*, 150.

30. Ibid., 28.

insight by demonstrating the way that being set in the way of love—the *ordo amoris*—allows us to respond rightly to the values in and of the world. For love reshapes the basic structure of our motivation, allowing us to respond from a whole heart to live rightly.

Scheler especially points out the way that being set in the *ordo amoris*, or not, sets our basic orientation in life. He does this through a meditation on Friedrich Nietzsche's term, *ressentiment*.[31] According to Scheler, *ressentiment* forms when we are injured—devalued in some way—by a person or group more powerful than us. Because of the injury, we come to devalue the values associated with the more powerful person or group. Who are they, that they are so important that they should hurt or devalue us? No one! On this basis, we come to despise the beings of those people and the good that they instantiate.

Ressentiment can become a way of life. Because we do not forgive, and because such wounds always come, the poison of *ressentiment* seeps through every aspect of our lives. It impairs our ability to make right value judgments, because our feelings become tinged with *ressentiment*. It becomes the dark undercurrent in our consciousness, leading us to make decisions we would never make otherwise, but which become sensible based on distorted responses to value.[32]

To take a somewhat ridiculous example, consider the character of Walter Sobchak, played by John Goodman in *The Big Lebowski*.[33] Walter is a veteran of the Vietnam War, living in 1990s Los Angeles. As the film proceeds from mildly crazy to wildly absurd, one of the consistent elements in the absurdity is Walter's ability to connect every situation he is in to the wrongs he experienced in that war. Whether dealing with rules violations in bowling, driving a van on the back roads of Orange County, having coffee with the movie's protagonist, fighting with a group of nihilists, or scattering the ashes of a dear friend, everything comes back to the devaluing of his person that he experienced in Vietnam.

In one memorable scene, Walter brandishes a service pistol at a fellow bowler whom he believes to have committed a rules violation. "Smokey, this is not Nam. This is bowling. There are rules," he says.[34] When Smokey refuses Walter's remonstrance, Walter threatens Smokey's

31. Frings, *Scheler*, 83.
32. Lonergan, *Method*, 33.
33. *The Big Lebowski*.
34. Ibid.

life. Because of his brutal experience of a world without rules in Vietnam, he has come to overvalue the rules of a game and devalue the worth of a human life. Walter has let *ressentiment* based on the devaluation he experienced become the basic existential fact of his life. Because of his dominating desire to express the value of his being, contrary to what he experienced, he is led to make decisions that are absurd. Walter's example is ridiculous, but it has comedic currency because it speaks to dynamics we know to be present in our lives. The wounds that we receive communicate to us a devaluing of our persons. Responding, we pay back wrong for wrong, seeking to validate ourselves.

The alternative to *ressentiment* is the way of love, and Scheler believed that we will live according to one of these two basic orientations. *Ressentiment* chooses to hold onto pain and try to overcome it through devaluing what truly is of value. Love chooses to overcome evil with good.

To return to Piaget's terms, *ressentiment* represents a block to the development of skills. It fixates one on the situations one has experienced and refuses the transformation of seeing the world and the other through the eyes of love. One's Being-in-the-World, rather than becoming more deeply intelligent and generous, becomes more and more absurd. Love, on the other hand, is a powerful dynamic for transformation. Following the way of love we exist in the world more authentically and in line with true value. The world is opened up to us in a new way because we ourselves have become greater within it.

In Maslow's terms, *ressentiment* might constitute a negative peak state. If peak experience allows one to live in a more self-transcendent and actualized way, *ressentiment* cuts one off from that life. In fact, it orients one toward a dis-value, causing the way one responds to the goodness and evil of the world to be distorted. Love, on the other hand, draws one to self-transcendence. The full term of love is found only in self-transcendence.

It is of immense importance for Lonergan that he considers that feelings can be educated.[35] They are, in fact, coordinated as skills. Feelings cannot, however, be educated *directly*. We simply cannot reach inside and change our hearts. It is possible, though, through affirmation and detestation, to affect the way we respond to the value of the world.

---

35. Lonergan, *Method*, 32.

To put it another way, it is possible to work oneself up to making a decision. What is required for a decision is simply an act of will—a choice. But it is not possible to work oneself up to falling in love. The responses we have to value are not completely under our control. They arise spontaneously. But through a slow process of self-discovery, affirming and reinforcing the feelings that cohere with our sense of values, and conversely refusing and negating those that do not, over time it is possible for the internal shape of our motivation to change.[36]

The role of community is of great importance for this process. An educational climate provides the resources for self-awareness and encouragement for those responses that truly are right. Likewise, we often come to know the darker parts of our being through our interaction with each other. It is part of the responsibility of the educational community to provide the resources and right standards for our moral education.

As Augustine pointed out, though, the transformation of our inner motivation on the basis of our own efforts alone faces an insurmountable problem. How do we have the moral compass to find the right way? And if our feelings are so distorted that we deeply need this change, why would we ever choose to undertake this long and difficult process? Does not our own history show us that humans have a great capacity for loving the darkness?

Lonergan (and Augustine and Aquinas) answered that it is not possible for us to change ourselves at the core in this way. But it is possible for God to make this change.[37] By the working of his grace, God can take our heart of stone and give us a heart of flesh. In fact, this is exactly the work Aquinas explained as sanctifying grace. Lonergan expresses this same reality as religious conversion. In religious conversion, the question of God becomes one that requires a decision on our part. We are placed within a new reality by grace and must choose whether to live a life that seeks out the source of the love that changes us.[38]

In religious conversion, we are both healed and elevated by grace.[39] The ground of *ressentiment* is shaken and a new logic of love can begin to take its place. And the orientation in love that we receive is to a love that is beyond merely human capacity. For the love that calls us is un-

36. Ibid.
37. Ibid., 33–34, 64.
38. Ibid., 116.
39. Ibid., 240–42.

restricted—never exhausted or satisfied by any finite thing but always calling us onward in love. If we respond authentically to this love—for we can refuse—our lives will change to match its shape and contour.

MORAL CONVERSION

Our basic moral commitment forms the vital crux between our intellectual being and the way we are transformed in love. Morality depends on feelings, too, because it involves intentional responses to value. Our ability rightly to value the world is of crucial import for our ability to live rightly in it. Truly moral living must come from our hearts.

Therefore, just as when following the path of wonder, we seek insights into the being of the world, so we also seek insights into the moral nature of the world.[40] These insights are affective; they come to us through the intentional responses to value that are feelings. Just as intellectual insights help us discover what is true about the world, affective insights help us discover what is truly worthwhile.

But beyond our ability to make right moral valuations is the question of whether we are truly committed to doing so. For it is possible to evaluate a system well with the intention of taking advantage of it. As discussed in the chapter on sin, the human person's orientation toward truth and the good can be deeply distorted.

With respect to this question, Lonergan speaks of moral conversion.[41] Just as intellectual conversion is a radical clarification of the human relation to truth, so moral conversion is a radical clarification of our relation to what is good. Just as religious conversion establishes in us dynamics of growth and the skills of love, so also moral conversion moves us toward virtue and justice.

The basic question of moral conversion is whether we are committed to the good in an absolute sense, or only in a restricted sense. In other words, do we truly care about the overall good, or do we pay most attention to our personal good, the good of our group, and to a short-sighted understanding of the good. If we falsely limit our consideration of what is worthwhile according to its effect on us (and those most like us), without consideration of wider points of view, we fail to seek and find the choices that are most worth making.

40. Ibid., 33–39.
41. Ibid., 240.

As with the other conversions, moral conversion is a sea change in the human spirit. We have, for example, a great ability to ignore questions and situations that might call us to personal sacrifice. In moral conversion, we choose that we will not limit our search for what is right in this way. Rather, we will be people of principle, who seek what is really of value and not merely what satisfies our own needs and point of view. Moral conversion does not make a life that is moral automatic; but growing into being a moral person will not be possible without this basis.

RELIGIOUS CONVERSION GROUNDS MORAL CONVERSION

Religious conversion inherently orders one to an unlimited good. God himself is the greatest good. In religious conversion, we are called and moved in love toward him. The horizon of our being has become transformed to love what we did not love before. In being called to the love of God, we are oriented within this horizon toward a good that exceeds the sum total of this world.

Religious conversion thereby provides a basis for the rectitude of our moral feelings. This world is created by God and shows the fingerprints of the Creator. Its every excellence shows the work of his hand and reflects his transcendent goodness. God is also, therefore, the good of every created good, for the meaning of every aspect of created being finds its true existence in rightly being related to him.

Religious conversion does not accomplish moral conversion, but it makes moral conversion both possible and probable.[42] Because religious conversion calls us to an unrestricted good (God), it becomes more probable that we will choose to seek what is good in an unrestricted way rather than being artificially restricted by our limited point of view. Religious conversion also makes it more probable that we will be able to find what is truly good, for the basic work of religious conversion reorders the world of our feelings. Because we are rewired inside, the logic our heart begins to follow becomes one that is more and more open to what truly is good.

To put it more technically, religious conversion causes a transformation in us whereby we develop affective skills.[43] This growth dynamic

42. Ibid., 243; see also Lonergan, "Moral Theology and the Human Sciences," 308.

43. Recall that "skills" means not tools that we can use but rather our very mode of being, existing wisely and lovingly in the world.

is properly ordered to God. In receiving this grace, we answer, "Yes," to the question that we are.[44] Because receiving this transformation means radically affirming the being that we have been given, it has strong implications for our being-in-the-world. On the basis of the affective skills that mark this transformation, we are directly ordered to the transcendent source of value.

Living authentically toward that transcendent source of value will involve a deep transformation in our concern. Because our concern has changed, our world has changed. Our horizon of expectation comes to include as a matter of first importance the overwhelming value of this transcendent love. Because our being-in-the-world becomes being-in-love, authenticity means something deeply different for us than it did before. It means living to eternal life, and it means this in a way that affirms this world. For because we have received an orientation in a horizon that is ordered to God in love, we are moved to be rightly ordered toward the world that God has made. This world resembles God in that it is his effect, and as we are changed by love it becomes possible, indeed probable, for us to consider this world as coming from and ordered to him. Because our living has become a decisive relationship with God, we are moved to love in his way and to love what he loves the more deeply we cooperate with him.

The right orientation provided by love makes it possible for us to be true to ourselves as moral beings. For it is the basic exigency of our moral being to live rightly. Because we are able to make responsible choices more regularly and on a true basis, we are more and more able to live authentically as ourselves. For, our own true self is not the self-denying life of irresponsible choices but rather the life of justice and love. Religious conversion establishes us in a horizon within which this life is possible. In moral conversion, we follow religious conversion's lead by choosing to value the world in a way that reflects its true value.

Moral conversion therefore makes possible and probable the overcoming of bias.[45] The noetic effects of sin, that have come to dominate our being, are overturned when we follow a logic of the heart that seeks

44. I thank Charles Hefling for this phrase.

45. Lonergan, *Method*, 270, deals with the healing of individual, group, and general bias. He does not discuss the healing of dramatic bias, or the bias of the unconscious motivations, directly, although he does indicate that the conversions are key; ibid., 231 and 231n107. We offer a possibly relevant application of the conversions to solving this deepest human issue.

what is truly good. Personal and group egoism are able to be transcended because we consider the good not just according to our own or our group's viewpoint. And the bias of shortsightedness is overcome because we do not limit the question of good temporally. Because moral conversion establishes the rectitude of our being with respect to what is truly worthwhile, it undercuts and frees us from the powerful effects of these engines of decline.

For moral conversion provides a basis for the right operation of our conscious intentionality. When we seek what is of value in the world, and try to choose responsibly, this is obviously a moral decision. But knowing the world is a moral act, too. To know the world we must be attentive to it, pay attention to and follow the drive of wonder in which we raise questions and seek to answer them. Because our knowledge of the world, considered from a fully human point of view, involves not just encountering the world but asking and answering these questions, the process of human knowledge is one that must be conducted on moral terms. It is we, as authentic beings, who are called to be attentive to the world, to seek to understand it intelligently, and come to reasonable judgments about it. Because moral conversion creates in us a basis for moral growth, it establishes growth dynamics in us that move us toward rectitude in all our conscious operations.

In moral conversion, we cooperate with God's grace in seeking and finding authentic human community. Without the grounding work of religious conversion, the essential logic of our hearts will remain prisoner to the darkness. Even freed of that domination, we are often ineffective in our search for what is good and true. But God's gift to us is not just himself but also our own true selves that we find in him. On the basis of his work of grace, we can—and are moved to—choose the goods in this world that are rightly ordered to him. And because his goodness is the origin and goal of every other good, we are thereby moved to make choices that discover what truly is of value and are motivated to choose those goods. Life in this world, then, life together, finds wholeness because together we are rightly ordered to God and the good.

A life lived faithfully to the gifts and choices of the conversions will be a life that operates according to the inner norms of its being, called forth and purified by love. Such a life radically transforms the meaning that we are, in a way that reaches to the inmost core of our being. In this way, it is possible to affect the root of radical sin within us, the bias of our unconscious motivations. No single conversion completely solves this deep problem. But as those transformed by love we receive the universal antecedent willingness that works to overcome even the darkness in our selves.

The task of overcoming this darkness is likely to be a long and arduous one, for our hearts so tellingly cling to our former way of life. The moral fortitude provided by moral conversion will be required, then. This should not be surprising. Overcoming the root of sin means setting right the basis of our motivation and desire.

And an implicit or explicit intellectual conversion seems necessary, too, for the work that we are called to do in overcoming this radical root involves first of all knowing ourselves and finding the meaning of our lives more truly in loving God than in being trapped in our allegiance to lesser desires. Whether or not one could articulate the awareness of intellectual conversion in philosophically adequate terms, one needs to see that we can know ourselves by knowing the meaning of our lives, and that we can change ourselves—and receive changes—by transformations of the meanings that constitute us.

Overcoming the radical root of sin in us will require the renewal and replacing of the symbols through which we understand God, the world, and ourselves. For symbols mediate between the world of explicit meaning and the world or the twilight of our consciousness, the world of feeling and affect. Intellectual conversion (implicit or explicit), moral conversion, and religious conversion provide the bases for our forming and receiving the new symbolic world through which we live in the world mediated by meaning, partially constituted by meaning, and motivated by value. In the renewing of our mind, we find a new language of the heart through the transformation of our aesthetic, symbolic, world and imagination.

PART THREE

Educating for Value

Authentic Humans and the Order of Love

6

Value Ethics

Forming Moral Agents

The full expression of our being, grounded by the conversions, comes through the life of love lived out in moral choices. As a way of understanding this life of self-transcendence, value ethics emerges from phenomenology in response to the inadequate theories of deontology and consequentialism. Authentic human agents, i.e., those who are intellectually, morally, and religiously converted, know, live, and act in the domain of values. Not only are they thus fully orbed and developed persons but are able to contribute to the world order, avoid decline, and contribute to the common good. This chapter is more theoretical than the subsequent one, and borrows from Taylor, Lonergan, Heidegger, as well as Max Scheler and John Paul II, to develop an account of moral authenticity.

DEONTOLOGY AND CONSEQUENTIALISM

Deontological and consequentialist ethics are the two main subdivisions of deontic ethical theory. Deontic ethical theories examine morality on the basis of the actions of the ethical subject. Their focus is on what we are supposed to do, or not do, in given practical situations. Both deontology and consequentialism themselves have a number of subdivisions: historical developments and attempts to address perceived weaknesses.

While this chapter cannot examine the variety of ethical theories thus produced, it will discuss the broad and overarching characteristics that apply to the various theories in these schools. Our intention is to show that value ethics provides a more successful account of human living that both avoids the main weaknesses of deontic ethics while satisfying its core concerns. In other words, our hope is not to refute but to "out-narrate" these competing ethical theories by showing that value ethics provides a basis for answering more of the relevant questions of human living, and answering those questions in a more satisfying way.[1]

Deontology emphasizes duty in conformity with moral norms.[2] In other words, no matter what the consequences, people in given situations are obligated to do certain things and not to do others. The criteria according to which these "certain things" and "others" are decided are moral principles or precepts that govern right behavior.

While the development of deontological ethical theory did not end with Immanuel Kant, no discussion of it can proceed very far without making reference to him.[3] As the paradigmatic deontologist, Kant set the agenda that subsequent schools of deontology follow. Kant analyzed moral action in terms of the moral intention of the agent according to or against the precepts provided by reason. He also emphasized an absolute moral worth of a person—human beings are ends, not means, and it is always immoral to treat them as tools through which one achieves one's ends rather than as intrinsically valuable in their own terms. In accord with this fundamental moral precept, Kant emphasized that one must choose those maxims that accord with every person's intrinsic rational nature, such as could be made a reasonable universal law.[4]

Consequentialism, to the contrary, insists that actions are right or wrong only on the basis of the consequences they have. While some types of consequentialism would try to include the motives of the acting parties in the ethical analysis, the rightness or wrongness of those motives can be decided, they say, solely on the basis of the results they produce. Consequentialism therefore attempts to assess actions based on the good produced or the evil prevented (or perhaps on a combined analysis of both).[5]

---

1. See Milbank, *Theology and Social Theory*, 380. See also Christopher Simpson's efforts along these lines with respect to core issues of deconstruction (Simpson, *Religion, Metaphysics, and the Postmodern*) and R. J. Snell's work treating Rorty's pragmatism (Snell, *Through a Glass Darkly*).

2. See Driver, *Ethics*, 80–81.

3. Ibid., 80–101.

4. Alexander and Moore, "Deontological Ethics."

5. See Driver, *Ethics*, 40–60, for classic utilitarianism and ibid., 61–79, for contemporary consequentialist ethics.

One finds the classic consequentialist theories in the utilitarian positions of Jeremy Bentham and John Stuart Mill.[6] While many modern consequentialist theories would hold a number of differences with Bentham and Mill, what they retain is an overall respect for utility, or subsequent goodness, as the standard according to which actions should be assessed. In other words, what is morally significant for an action is what follows from it rather than anything leading up to it, such as a moral precept according to which a decision should be made.

To see the differences between these two schools of deontic ethics, consider the ethical dilemma faced by Sydney Carton at the end of Dickens' *Tale of Two Cities*.[7] Carton is a barrister during the time leading up to the French Revolution. As established in the book, he bears a strong physical resemblance to another character, a disgraced French aristocrat Charles Darnay. Significantly, Darnay throughout the book has pursued moral courses of action in distancing himself from his brutal aristocratic heritage and showing compassion for the state of the poor. Carton, to the contrary, is by all accounts a perpetually inebriated ne'er-do-well; in fact, though he has acted in Darnay's favor on one occasion, Carton despises Darnay as a symbol of Carton's own lost potential. To complete the conflict between the two, both men end up pledging their love to the same woman, Lucie Manette. When Darnay is successful in his pursuit of Lucie, Carton eventually requests their friendship, promising his own in return.

At the climax of the book, Darnay returns from the relative safety of England to a situation of great risk in revolutionary France. His intention is to save a man unjustly accused of murdering Darnay's uncle. Return to France carries great risks, for all aristocrats were subject to suspicion and arrest during the Revolution. Darnay is indeed arrested, falsely charged, and condemned to die. The plot against him finally grows to include grave risk to his wife and child. Carton has travelled to Paris with the idea of rescuing Darnay, but is faced with grave difficulty due to the high-profile nature of Darnay's "crimes" and imprisonment. Carton, also, comes to know the threat against Lucie and her child.

Given this situation, what should Carton do? Or more precisely, how should Carton analyze this ethical situation and the potential actions he might undertake within it? As the book ends, is he right that,

6. See Sinnott-Armstrong, "Consequentialism."
7. Dickens, *Tale of Two Cities*.

"It is a better thing that now I do than I have ever done?" And is that so because, "It is a better rest to which I go than I have ever known," or would it be the case irrespective of that consequence? Deontological ethics would ask Carton about his duty, either to himself, or to Darnay and his family, or to society, or to some combination of the above. It would also remind Carton that Darnay and Lucie (as well as he, himself) are intrinsically valuable moral subjects and cannot rightly be reduced to the means to his personal satisfaction. Finally, it would ask Carton how universally applicable the course of action he chooses would be. In other words, would Carton find his actions reasonable if the tables were turned, or if everyone started acting in this way?

What deontological ethics would not ask Carton, though, is to consider the consequences of his actions; or to be more precise, it would not ask him to do so in a way that could trump the requirements of duty. Consequentialism, though, asks Carton precisely this question, to the exclusion of considerations of the prior claims of duty. What, the consequentialist would ask, does Carton expect to occur based on rescuing or not rescuing Darnay? Will happiness or utility or good be maximized? Will pain or evil be avoided? Will the good that is sought be universally applicable, or only a private good (and therefore less valuable).

It is interesting to consider how either kind of ethics would analyze Carton's solution of drugging Darney in his cell in the Bastille, blackmailing a corrupt British spy to sneak the unconscious Darnay out of the prison, and then taking Darnay's place (recall the strong physical resemblance between the two) to face the guillotine. Likely, both consequentialists and deontologists would find different aspects of Carton's actions to be praiseworthy and blameworthy. Deontologists would find the choice to remove Darnay as an effective moral agent (by drugging him), committing blackmail, breaking the law of the land by helping a convicted criminal escape, and multiple episodes of lying to be problematic as fulfillments of duty. However, they might praise Carton's will to keep his promise of friendship and save an innocent life. Consequentialists, contrarily, would ask about the results flowing from Carton's choice. Is the loss of his life and happiness compensated for by a greater good, or for the significant good of a greater number of people? Do the actions of drugging a person and committing blackmail increase or decrease the overall utility or good present in the situation?

THE FORGOTTEN MORAL SUBJECT AND VIRTUE ETHICS

What neither deontological nor consequentialist ethics do, however, is ask Carton who he is as a moral agent making this decision. Carton's moral being is considered only in terms of extrinsic factors, either duties that come from beyond him or consequences that extend beyond him. This forgetfulness of the person is intrinsic to deontic ethics, for the basis of ethical consideration is explicitly the behavior, not the person. They are about what we are supposed to do—but who are we? The rightness or wrongness of Carton's character and Carton's relation as a person to what is good and true do not fall within the purview of deontic ethics.

But it is of central importance to any analysis of moral decision making that *people* make the evaluations, and *people* live out the situations (not ethical principles or consequences of actions). Virtue ethics reemerged in modern ethical debate partly due to dissatisfaction with the forgetfulness of the subject characteristic of deontic ethics.[8]

> Neither [deontology nor consequentialism], at that time, paid attention to a number of topics that had always figured in the virtue ethics' tradition—the virtues themselves, motives and moral character, moral education, moral wisdom or discernment, friendship and family relationships, a deep concept of happiness, the role of the emotions in our moral life and the fundamentally important questions of what sort of person I should be and how we should live.[9]

While subsequent iterations of deontological and consequentialist ethics have attempted to remedy some of these lacunae, virtue ethics has these questions as its primary focus.[10]

Deontological ethics questions Carton's duties, and consequentialism reminds him to consider the results of his actions, but neither asks him, "Sydney Carton, who are you?" Carton's identity and person, again, are considered as null factors by these theories. Deontic ethics specifies behavior, not persons. Neither deontic theory has a clear way to link moral action with personal identity and moral character. Nor do they seem to have an adequate basis for consideration of a radical change in a person's ethical basis of operation.

8. See Anscombe, "Modern Moral Philosophy", 1–19.
9. Rosalind Hursthouse, "Virtue Ethics."
10. See Driver, *Ethics*, 136–153.

We would argue that a full-orbed ethical analysis will take into account the duties a person has as well as the consequences of her actions. Yet the basis for doing so will be found in the ethical being of the responsible person. Furthermore, the authenticity of this person—the basis for right analysis of right behavior—serves as the criterion by which truly ethical behavior can be known. For to live ethically means to be true to oneself as one has been transformed, converted with respect to truth, goodness, and love.

VIRTUE ETHICS AS MORAL THEORY

Virtue ethics formally emerged in the ancient ethical tradition with the writings of Plato and Aristotle.[11] It is a point of view that came to characterize the great bulk of ancient and medieval ethical thought. While it suffered a loss of popularity during and subsequent to the Enlightenment, it reemerged as a major ethical viewpoint in the 20th century.

In contrast to deontic ethics, virtue ethics insists that the first requisite for moral action is the establishment of a moral character in the person. While virtue ethics does specify many aspects of behavior, it sees ethical action as flowing from a rightly shaped inner moral being. To use an apt metaphor, "First clean the inside of the cup and the plate, that the outside also may be clean."[12] Most schools of virtue ethics traditionally consider this congruence between inner rightness and right behavior under the headings of *aretē* (excellence, or virtue), *phronêsis* (prudence, or practical wisdom), and *eudaimonia* (happiness, or flourishing).

Aretē refers to the embodied and enacted excellence of the human spirit. Usually translated as "virtue," *aretē* describes what it means for human potential to be achieved in its most positive way. This excellence must be thoroughgoing, involving the character of the person as expressed in the actions that person takes. Character—a stable disposition to act in a certain way—therefore grounds personal morality and gives the person's actions moral consistency and value.

Virtue ethics analyzes human character traits in ways that are connected but differentiated. The most common organization of the moral virtues would involve character traits of justice, temperance, fortitude, and practical wisdom. The basic premise of virtue ethics is that who and

---

11. Hursthouse, "Virtue Ethics."
12. Matthew 23:26 (ESV).

what we are affects what we are able or likely to do, and that our inner moral character is therefore the basis of our moral (or immoral) action. These actions, as moral, do not tend to be random but reflect either stable moral dispositions or the lack of those dispositions.

For example, one may find that the people who don't cheat on their taxes also tend not to embezzle money from work. In this case, they could be understood to manifest a basic character trait of honesty in two different situations. If these same people tend to make their word their bond, have a regard for the rights of others, and live in submission to just forms of government, we would tend to see a character trait of justice in them. That is, these people, by acting justly in a number of various situations, evidence a stable disposition of justice according to which they make moral choices and avoid immoral ones.

Just as different sets of actions are coordinated by the analysis of virtue ethics under the stable dispositions indicated by the Cardinal virtues, so the action of the virtues themselves is tested and ordered by *phronêsis*. *Phronêsis* usually is translated as "prudence" or "practical wisdom." It is the chief of the moral virtues, being itself a moral virtue and also regulating the other moral virtues. *Phronêsis* involves the ability to know both what is best to do in practical situations and also the best means to achieve those ends.

It is extremely important not to see practical wisdom as a set of tools that a prudent person can use. "Tools" seem to be value neutral. They are also disconnected from the identity and nature of the person who uses them. Under this analysis, prudence could seem to imply simply the ability to "get things done" in a given situation, irrespective of whether those things are wise or not. It also seems that prudence makes no difference for the identity and character of the person. If you have a tool, or do not have it, you are essentially the same; your action in the situations you find yourself in would not reveal something essential about you.

But practical wisdom in reality shows the way that we are able or unable to live intelligently and reasonably in the situations in which we exist. It is we, ourselves, as we understand our world rightly and operate in it wisely. A person who knows how to exist well in the world because he has come to understand it well does not just possess a valuable tool. Rather, that person has developed a stable disposition of wisdom with respect to practical affairs.

In any serious consideration of justice one comes up against the question of how one finds the appropriate balance between leniency and stringency in applying laws and standards. Similarly, any examination of fortitude must be able to tell the difference between bravery and rashness, and discretion and cowardice, before it can be of much value. Temperance, likewise, must find the right balance between a pusillanimous and a profligate disposition. But how can they do so?

It is the function of practical wisdom to find the right balance in these cases.[13] For a person of practical wisdom knows the difference. In fact, one could even consider that justice, temperance, and fortitude flow from practical wisdom. For they are stable dispositions to relate rightly to reality in different respects, and it is the nature of practical wisdom to know what these right relations are. In this way prudence does not replace justice, fortitude, and temperance, but it provides the basis for their existence and regulates their function as true human excellences.

Virtue ethicists would argue that moral human action is not random but rather proceeds with purpose toward a goal.[14] This goal is usually defined as *eudaimonia*. If *aretē* and *phronêsis* offer pitfalls in their translation, *eudaimonia* sends one through a veritable minefield. The most usual translation is "happiness," although "flourishing" may come closer to expressing the heart of the word.

Perhaps the simplest way to gauge *eudaimonia's* meaning is to ask, "If a person has stable dispositions of virtue and lives out practical wisdom, what is supposed to be the result?" Because the virtues instantiate the excellences of the human spirit, with practical wisdom being their ground and crown in moral terms, *eudaimonia* will express that state of excellence reached by a human being who truly follows the way of virtue. The "happiness" virtue ethicists speak of, therefore, is an objective state that encapsulates what it means to be a human being living rightly in the world, whose excellence runs all the way through, being grounded in a moral character and expressing itself in action.

Virtue ethicists would vary concerning the role that external circumstances play in a person's happiness. Some, for instance, would argue that a person who experiences a disaster and whose life ends in ruin should not be considered a "happy" person even if she has developed and lived out a sterling moral character. In other words, the heart of the

13. See Pieper, *Brief Reader on the Virtues of the Human Heart*, 11–12.
14. *ST* I-II 1.1.

matter is one's character as lived out in the world, but the circumstances in which one does so may or may not allow one truly to achieve "happiness" or "flourishing." Others would argue that the most significant aspects of human flourishing involve precisely the way a person's character develops and is expressed, and that the circumstances in which one lives do not have the ability to cancel out that excellence. By this analysis, even someone whose life seems to end in ruin could be considered "happy," because the objective analysis of her character and action shows what an excellent human being in her situation should aspire to be and do. In any case, no virtue ethicist would simply equate *eudaimonia* with the transitory and purely emotional state indicated by "happiness" in modern English. *Eudaimonia*, in fact, indicates what it means for all things human truly to be well.

While he was not the first virtue ethicist, Aristotle is as paradigmatic for virtue ethics as Kant for deontological. Aristotle's *Nicomachean Ethics* remains to this day a seminal text in this tradition. In this work, *aretē*, *phronêsis*, and *eudaimonia* receive searching explanations, along with continence, distributive and retributive justice, friendship, self-love, the right distribution of human life between action and philosophical contemplation, and the nature of ethical analysis itself. While Aristotle by no means begins or ends the virtue ethics conversation, subsequent virtue ethicists have found in his work a contribution of enduring value.

By returning to the question of Sidney Carton, we can see the way that virtue ethics takes into account the concerns of both deontological and consequentialist ethics. Because virtue ethics sees justice as a cardinal moral character trait, it includes the question of Catron's duty in the moral analysis. Because all moral character centrally involves practical wisdom, virtue ethics also takes account of the consequences of Catron's actions. But it places both of these questions in the context of what it is truly human to do. In other words, by asking questions of justice and prudence, virtue ethics is more fundamentally asking Carton the question of who he is as a moral agent acting in this situation. Insofar as he lives up to the character of a wise and just man, Carton acts morally in the world; that is, he instantiates what it means to be a person of excellence making practically wise—and therefore excellent—choices in his situation.

Because virtue ethics makes character of central importance, it is capable of dealing with change of character in a way that deontic ethics of either stripe cannot. Throughout the progress of *A Tale of Two Cities*, Carton has changed. A key point in the change probably occurs when he promises friendship to Darnay and Lucie. The culmination of this change takes place when he follows through with this promise, arranging for their escape from France at the cost of his life. The behavior that Carton evidences would have a fundamentally different meaning without this change of character. Instead of having a depraved will that occasionally and sporadically does good, Carton has experienced a transformation in his moral basis. The moral character of his actions in saving Lucie and Darnay consists in the congruity of his behavior with this new moral basis—a reformed, or converted, will. In other words, the deed he does in saving Darnay is better than any other he has done not just because of its cost or effects but because he is a new man in doing it. And the better rest to which he goes indicates the integrity of being and life that he has found thereby.

VALUE ETHICS

Virtue ethics, as developed by Aristotle and extended by Augustine and Aquinas, uses the categories and thought forms of Aristotle's ancient faculty psychology (first act, second act, will, intellect, appetites, etc.). Value ethics attempts to take the central insights of virtue ethics and transpose them into thought forms informed by modern phenomenology and psychology. Thus, where virtue ethics speaks of character traits in terms of habits that the virtuous person has or forms, value ethics would perform the same ethical analysis based on the values that the subject evidences, pursues, and instantiates.

Virtues are habits that cohere in the person as a second nature. Values indicate the growth transformation of the subject in forming moral and intellectual skills (re: Piaget and Maslow). Values also indicate the being of the subject in a transformed horizon; they especially speak of how intellectual, moral, and religious conversion transform and order the subject's being-in-the-world (re: Heidegger, Taylor, and Lonergan).

Value ethics, in continuity with virtue ethics, also emphasizes that the moral action of the subject coheres with sets of immanent norms. Just as the intellectually converted subject follows the intrinsic call of wonder by which she is an intelligent and reasonable being, so also the morally converted subject follows the intrinsic call of value by which she is a responsible being. True moral behavior comes from the heart and is lived out in a world intelligently understood and reasonably assessed.

Value ethics (in contrast to many deontic ethics), though, is capable of receiving an external standard for behavior such as a legal code or a divine command. What it will maintain, though, is that any such legitimate standard will be calling the subject to a new way of being, not just an external form of behavior. Value ethics will furthermore expect legitimate external standards to express the moral nature of the order of the universe.[15] By directing the subject to congruity with this order, the legitimate external standard is in fact directing her to the right fulfillment of the immanent moral norms of her being.

Centrally, then, value ethics points to the transformation of the subject's feelings. Feelings indicate the way our beings are motivated with respect to values. When our character shows the fruit of intellectual, moral, and religious conversions, we are more likely to respond to that which truly is worthwhile and do so in an ordered and appropriate way. This is so because we ourselves have become more rightly ordered to it, having a more authentic basis by which to form assessments of truth and value.

One of the most provoking and searching affirmations of virtue ethics is Augustine's dictate, "Love, and do what you will."[16] Deontic ethical theorists would strenuously protest this maxim; it specifies nothing in terms of duty or consequences of actions, but only a transformed will regulated by love. How can it be realistic to tell any human will, "Do what you want?" The secret is that truly ethical behavior flows from immanent norms, namely, the transformed character of the human person. Insofar as the human character bears out and is authentic to this transformation (religious conversion, in Lonergan's terms), the desires it has (its feelings) will cohere with what truly is of value, and that the subject desires to do will in fact tend to be right.

At least, the desires will tend to cohere with a right valuation of the world as far as the subject understands it. Right knowledge of the world, and especially human reality, will then be essential for truly moral behavior. On other words, value ethics does not dispense with prudence

---

15. In this respect, value ethics calls for a transposition of natural law theory. For a powerful first step in this process, see Lonergan, "Natural Right and Historical Mindedness," 169–183.

16. Augustine, "Homily 7 on the First Epistle of John."

but rather sees the wisdom indicated by it as a necessary grounding of moral action. Yet prudence does not necessarily indicate the rectitude of one's heart.

Augustine was a pastor, having active responsibility for the cure of souls. He had a quite realistic understanding of how far a human subject would need to be transformed in order to be pure in heart. But what it will mean for a human subject truly to be ethical—truly to be human—through and through will be for his heart's desire to conform to what is good and true, and then to live authentically and wisely in the world in conformity with that desire.

The only right basis for this conformity is transformation of the subject's heart by the love of God (see Romans 5:5). Augustine saw the need for this basis on two grounds. First, human beings were always created to be in relation to God; living in loving relation to God is the intended fulfillment of our being. Second, the effects of sin dominate human beings in their current state. The root of this domination is disordered love (concupiscence). To have our disordered love replaced by love of God means to be restored to right human being by God's grace. Only God's love is the right basis for human living, for we are made in God's image and for right relation with him.[17]

In Lonergan's terms, then, religious conversion transforms our being-in-the-world into being-in-love, setting us in a horizon in which we are ordered to and by the love of God. On the basis of religious conversion, we are able to know the value of the world in a new way (a right way), for God's love calls us in an unrestricted way. This new way involves the transformation of our feelings by which the structure of our motivation comes to reflect the ordering of God's love. We come therefore to live more authentically in the world because the values we respond to are more and more values that are true. When this new way of loving captures us, we are more likely to receive and choose a more authentic moral basis (moral conversion), in which we live authentically to the values in the world because we are motivated to seek that which is truly of value (and not just satisfying for us or good from a restricted point of view).

While the transformation of value and feeling will not necessarily be received or understood by the subject in religious, or even philosophical, terms, it will move the subject to a transformed way of being

17. Augustine, *Confessions*, 1.1.

in some terms of central importance to that person. But all religions and philosophies (and most other wide-ranging points of view such as political commitments) make fundamental claims about the nature and value of the world. Because the subject has experienced a transformation of meaning and value either in those terms or by adopting new terms, he has been equipped to recognize more fully the nature of truth in the world mediated by meaning. On the basis of the transformations of moral and religious conversion, then, the subject is enabled and made likely to come to an intellectually converted viewpoint.

At the heart of all these transformations is love. Converted by and for love, set by love on a transformed moral basis, ordered by love to discover rectitude in knowing truth, authentic human being radiates from and is fulfilled by love. On the basis the authentic feelings that are prompted and communicated by and in love, the human subject lives in the realms of value in a new, truly real, way.

AUTHENTIC HUMAN BEING

John Paul II's theology of the body offers a powerful understanding of authentic human being coherent with the explanation of value ethics. While he develops many of these themes from his doctoral dissertation (on Max Scheler) onward, his catechetical work, *Man and Woman He Created Them: A Theology of the Body*, offers a *locus classicus* of this aspect of his thought.[18] In this work, John Paul begins with the creation account and proceeds to examine carefully the Biblical teaching on authentic human subjectivity and marriage.

Richard Grecco analyzes John Paul's teaching on sexuality according to three points: 1) It offers theological reflection, not mere rules; 2) It is phenomenological—paying attention to experience—and not an abstract deduction from natural law theory; 3) This emphasis on subjectivity eschews rationalism (although not rationality) and adverts to modes of knowing such as body language, spontaneity, and intimacy.[19] One can see the power of this method clearly in the way that John Paul analyzes the objective nature of the subjectivity of love.

18. John Paul II, *Man and Woman.*
19. Grecco, "Recent Ecclesiastical Teaching," 146.

According to *Man and Woman*, married life is an "evangelical vocation."[20] It has this character precisely as a mode by which present human beings, suspended and living between the two poles of creation and final, eschatological, redemption, can come to live with courage and wisdom leading to life. Precisely because of the struggles that often attend married life, and also due to its joys, married life forms a way in which faith and hope become real based on the love that God has poured into our hearts (Romans 5:5).[21]

Christopher West, in his insightful commentary on *Man and Woman*, expresses John Paul's meaning this way:

> Notice how the Pope, in the following definition of love, links subjectivity with objective truth. He states that, "*love*, from the subjective viewpoint, is a *power* ... given to man in order to participate in that love with which God himself loves in the mystery of creation and redemption" (406). In other words, love has an anchor. It has an objective reference point. That reference point is Ultimate Truth itself: for *God is love* (1 Jn 4:8).[22]

What it means for men and women to live in loving marriage together is to reflect, in their action and being, the community of love that the Triune God is.

John Paul repeatedly refers to the way that this reality of human existence is grounded in Creation.[23] In many of these references, he analyzes the way that the Genesis account reveals and explains human subjectivity.[24] This nascent but complete human subjectivity included self-consciousness and self-determination. It also, quite significantly, included covenantal life with God, in which human subjectivity includes and means our inclusion in a relationship with God. What it means to grow into ourselves—to have a complete human subjectivity—is to grow in all of these objectively valid ways.

---

20. John Paul II, *Man and Woman*, 641 (126:4).

21. Ibid., (126:4–5).

22. West, *Theology of the Body Explained*, 444.

23. According to its Scripture index, *Man and Woman* refers to Genesis 1 sixty-eight times. It refers to Genesis 2 at least twice as many times. John Paul II, *Man and Woman*, 725.

24. For example, see his comments on "Solitude and Subjectivity," in John Paul II, *Man and Woman*, 150–51 (6:1).

Human existence, grounded in Creation, has its inherent and expected culmination in the Life of the World to Come.[25] In this way, human morality flows from the objective value present in human being. For human being, as it is created to be, is a historical progress that will overstep the bounds of the present world. And to live authentically to human being means to live out love, the love that never fails, and that bears the stamp of the very character of God.

CONCLUSION

The point of value ethics is to show the way that the converted subject's transformed heart and mind bear fruit in the way that she lives. The presence or absence of conversion has consequences, not first of all in whether she lives up to a given standard of morality but rather in terms of whether she lives up to being her own human self. Religious, moral, and intellectual conversions indicate the basis of genuine subjectivity and authenticity: a life in which right choices reflect a transformed life dedicated to truth, goodness, and love.

John Paul II's theology of marriage shows the way that the basic relationships of human existence become evangelical vocations. In other words, for human living truly to cohere to the call of the conversions, as explained by value ethics, the concrete situations of our lives must be transformed by truth, goodness, and love. While we are called to the requirements of duty and must consider the import and consequences of our actions, the first question for ethics is who we are as ethical beings and the last question is how that ethical being becomes factical in history. The conversions indicate not academic jargon, but a transformed way of life. This chapter has explained the way that conversion grounds a real and viable ethics and showed a first example in which, in a core relationship, the way that we are ethical beings (or not) radically shapes the character and tenor of our existence. Our next chapter expands that explanation to encompass the cosmopolitan nature of authentic human life.

25. Note eighteen references in *Man and Woman* to the Resurrection Chapter, 1 Corinthians 15.

7

Cosmopolis

Value, Justice, Authenticity

The anthropology of love articulated in previous chapters is here pulled together into an account of progress, decline, and redemption in history. Since subjectivity is always socially and historically engaged, involved in projects of value and concern, it would be quite inadequate to overlook the human good and the barriers and impediments of its achievement. Further, claiming that sin and grace are not abstractions but actually operative in subjectivity demands extending our previous discussions of bias and conversion into the realm of community and history, for if subjectivity is factical, and if sin and grace operate concretely in subjectivity, then sin and grace will be factical as well, found in concrete reality in history and community.

Further, given Lonergan's own concern to include historicity in philosophic method, and his further concern for Christian thought to rise to the level of the times rather than remain in systems of the past, we place an important element of Lonergan's thought on historical development, a notion he terms *cosmopolis*, into the context of contemporary cosmopolitanism; if the human good is not an abstraction but a historical development, our account must be in conversation with the historical situation, which now includes a revival of cosmopolitanism in the way we apprehend the human good. Lonergan's account, moreover, articulates the barriers to genuine value and its apprehension, and so indicates the necessity of religious value for achieving the human good, a necessity at the very core of the cosmopolitan predicament. While cosmopolis and cosmopolitanism are not identical, the role of cosmopolis in reversing decline, and its ultimate impotence to overthrow the reign

146

of sin, reveals something of real import for the hopes of human development and flourishing.

RENAISSANCE OF AN IDEAL

While cosmopolitanism is an ancient ideal, contemporary articulations have developed under the influence, among other things, of globalization, postmodern concern for the "other," post-colonialism, and post-national understandings of citizenship.[1] While the notion and the scholarship surrounding it are likely meaningful for a "rather small segment of cultural elites ... explicit appeal to cosmopolitan ideals is, for an elite minority, no longer merely a figurative and abstract gesture, but ostensibly a very literal possibility for the first time in human history."[2] For a variety of reasons, a large number of contemporary thinkers favor cosmopolitan understandings of justice, citizenship, identity, and its concomitant post-national institutions and imagination, although detractors note the potentially undemocratic nature of cosmopolitanism, its hostility to place, tradition, and community, its cultural elitism, and the odd contradiction of a universal vision which is really that of a progressive European Enlightenment overlooking real diversity and particular identity.[3]

The term *kosmopolites*, or citizen of the world, is attributed to Diogenes Laertius, although Diogenes thought the cosmopolitan was somewhat homeless, "rather than being at home in *every* city, they were *indifferent* to them *all*."[4] In denouncing local community, the Cynics rejected that which was conventional (*nomos*) as an element of their radical break from social normalcy in favor of a way of life of complete independence which they viewed as natural (*phusis*) and superior.[5] In doing so, the distinction between what was right by nature as opposed to mere (local) convention was made paramount, and the Cynic bequeathed a spirit of critical reflexivity allowing a distantiation from their

1. For a discussion of classical and contemporary versions, see Delanty, *Cosmopolitan Imagination*, 18–88. See also Appiah, *Cosmopolitanism*; Seyla Benhabib, *Another Cosmopolitanism*; Keys, *Aquinas, Aristotle, and the Promise of the Common Good*.

2. Yates, "Mapping the Good World," 7, 8.

3. For a bibliographic essay with summary of the positions, see Dill, "Cosmopolitanism," 125–33.

4. Benhabib, "Cosmopolitanism and Democracy," 32.

5. Hadot, *Ancient Philosophy*, 109–10.

regime not entirely dissimilar from contemporary cosmopolitans for whom " . . . boundaries, including state borders and frontiers, require moral justification."[6]

After the Cynics, the Stoics developed cosmopolitanism in its most familiar direction. Attempting to articulate rational principles for political community, they turned to the universalism of reason rather than the rejection of lived political and social life, tending to expand political participation and in an Empire covering multiple regions and religions.[7] Marcus Aurelius, the Emperor, claims that if humans "have intelligence in common, so we have reason. . . . If so, then the law is also common to us and, if so, we are citizens . . . we share a common government . . . the universe is, as it were, a city."[8]

Stoics incorporated their universalist view of reason into the natural law and its claims of equality: "Slaves, too, are men, blood relations and brethren. . . . The city-state has thus lost its power, and with it has disappeared the differentiation of mankind into Greeks and barbarians, into freeman and slaves."[9] This higher law tradition transcends the positive laws of regimes and provides an account of what is just by nature, a system furthered by Aquinas, the medieval canon lawyers, and influencing early modern accounts of natural law and natural rights.[10] Modern thought is most closely identified with what could be termed "classical cosmopolitanism," with three defining traits: (1) a tradition of humanism and civic republicanism centered on moral and political unity, especially as evidenced by international law; (2) a cosmopolitanism of science and letters, shared in common by those of broad and cultivated education; (3) an encounter with cultures and texts from beyond the West.[11] These traits are perhaps most evident in the thought of Immanuel Kant.

Kant's moral theory allows autonomous individuals to formulate the moral law for themselves, and to be duty-bound to no moral imperative they would not in principle give to themselves; but given the universality of reason, duties are also universal and so bind all persons equally in a universal kingdom. While all are free under their own reason,

6. Benhabib, *Another Cosmopolitanism*, 19.

7. Delanty, *Cosmopolitan Imagination*, 20–24.

8. In Benhabib, "Cosmopolitanism and Democracy," 32.

9. Rommen, *Natural Law*, 21–22.

10. Ibid., 30–96.

11. Delanty, *Cosmopolitan Imagination*, 30.

moral laws are necessary, apodictic, and universally compelling.[12] In two essays—"Idea for a Universal History with a Cosmopolitan Purpose," and "Perpetual Peace"—Kant argues for a cosmopolitan vision of free republican states developing their legal structures in a way conducive to moral development rather than mere self-interest, with freedom for all, a common law, and legal equality before the law.[13] Furthermore, universal moral community required rightful relations between states as well as the cosmopolitan duty of hospitality which includes the right of the non-citizen to access and dwell temporarily in other states.[14]

The cosmopolitan spirit of the Enlightenment collapses before nationalism, to be revived in recent decades, thought by some an ideal genuinely to be sought and instantiated. In some ways, the more traditional questions of "What is the good life?" and "What is the good society?" have been transposed into the "problem of the good world," with the problem opening "a new chapter full of strife and controversy over the very meaning of the good *world* and, significantly, who gets to define it."[15] Perceptions of the abuses and cultural arrogance of Enlightenment thought pose something of a problem for cosmopolitanism, and, consequently, contemporary versions promote "a (post) universalistic ethic that is better suited to the empirical realities of global change, but most importantly to the enduring human need for particularistic attachments," and take into account the variety of experiences of the cosmopolitans themselves.[16] Consequently, "there is explicit resistance to attaching any determinate meaning to the term," and accounts are open, adjectival, variegated, and in flux.[17]

Despite hesitations on the pedigree of cosmopolitanism, a sense of its indispensability remains, with many theorists and practitioners articulating a profound need to form a cosmopolitan outlook, or, even, that such a vision is already formed, that we already picture a singular, unified world waiting for moral systems and institutions to catch up to our imagination—for thought to catch up to love, in a way.[18]

12. See Arkes, *First Things*.
13. Ibid., 32–33.
14. Benhabib, *Another Cosmopolitanism*, 21–23.
15. Yates, "Mapping the Good World," 8.
16. Ibid., 9. See also Matustík, "Democratic Multicultures and Cosmopolis," 63–89.
17. Ibid.
18 Ibid., 11–16.

PROGRESS, DECLINE, AND REDEMPTION

The argument below depends substantially on previous chapters, for authentic cosmopolitanism, as we articulate it, is an account of authentic subjectivity attained through intellectual, moral, and religious conversion. Bias and the disorders of sin impede cosmopolis, and while subjects can move towards authenticity from the basis of their own development and achievement, in the end sin and decline are undone and overcome only through redemption and the ordering of subjectivity by grace, especially through the love of God poured out into human hearts. Cosmopolis, then, is primarily about *value*, about love, in bringing about authenticity and genuine self-transcendence.

The Human Good

While cosmopolis is not primarily about education, Lonergan first uses the term in a treatise on education, "The Role of a Catholic University in the Modern World," explaining the isomorphism between consciousness and the human good. In his account, just as human knowing involves experience, understanding, and judgment, so the human good involves objects of desire, the good of order, and value.[19] Human community follows a similar pattern, with particular goods corresponding to inter-subjective community, the good of order corresponding to civil society and civilization, and value corresponding to cultural community; this cultural community is cosmopolis:

> Corresponding to judgments of value, there is cultural community. It transcends the frontiers of states and the epochs of history. It is cosmopolis, not as an unrealized political ideal, but as a longstanding, nonpolitical, cultural fact. It is the field of communication and influence of artists, scientists, and philosophers. It is the bar of enlightened public opinion to which naked power can be driven to submit. It is the tribunal of history that may expose successful charlatans and may restore to honor the prophets stoned by their contemporaries.[20]

While that definition provides some context for our inquiry, it will not have much significance without explicating Lonergan's account of the human good and the dialectics of progress, decline, and redemption.

19. Lonergan, "Role of a Catholic University in the Modern World," 108–9.
20. Ibid., 109.

While those themes recur throughout his work, the 1959 Cincinnati lectures on Education, *Topics in Education*, clearly link cosmopolis and education. *Topics in Education* navigates several disputes between traditionalists and modernists in the Roman Catholic educational context at mid-century.[21] After summarizing the situation, the substance of the lectures begins with a discussion of the human good, for if the goal is to "provide a basis for . . . discussion of the end, the aim, the goal of education," and if education seeks some good, then understanding the good would be the first order of business.[22] Not the good of education specifically, but the human good *per se*.

Coming to terms with the good is tricky, for the good, like being, is comprehensive, not reducible to one mode of reality or set of categories, but relating to every mode, for there are good substances, good quantities, good relations, good places, good events, good qualities, and so on. Consequently, while the good is comprehensive, it is not abstract, less like Plato's Good and more like Aristotle's.[23] Further, the good is not merely one aspect of things, "as though the rest of their reality were evil," nor is it a negation—don't do this, or that!—or a double negation—not evil—although it is "not apart from evil in this life."[24] The good is not an ideal, either, for it "is in things; it is something existing," and it exists not as a static blueprint but as an ongoing and dynamic process of human intelligence and action.[25] Lonergan articulates the *human* good, and as human it is factical and historical, "realized though human apprehension and choice," thus "[i]t is a history, a concrete, cumulative process resulting from developing human apprehension and human choices that may be good or evil."[26] As a side note, this is one of the rare texts placing evil and sin at the very center of education, with *progress, decline*, and *redemption* serving as *the* central categories; if the good is historical, we should not be surprised to find evil, sin, and redemption in an account of education.

While the human good develops historically, there is an invariant structure, appropriated through reflexive exegesis, even when the

21. Lonergan, *Topics in Education*.
22. Ibid., 26.
23. Ibid., 28.
24. Ibid., 28–29.
25. Ibid., 29–30.
26. Ibid., 32–33.

transcendental invariance is *always* conditioned by the concrete and entirely variable realities of persons in their places and times—while we are dealing with concrete subjects in their facticity rather than with a fixed human nature, subjectivity has its invariants. In *Topics in Education* Lonergan identifies three main aspects of the human good—the particular good, the good of order, and value, although these are expanded and articulated somewhat differently in later work as vital, social, cultural, personal, and religious values.[27] Particular good (vital value) regards the satisfaction of a discrete appetite; the good of order (social value) is a system for the "flow of particular goods" and includes "a regular recurrence of particular goods, coordinated human operations, a set of conditions of these operations, and personal status."[28] From the more compact articulation in *Topics*, value is broken into aesthetic, ethical, and religious types.

History and the Possibility of Decline

While the structure just sketched is invariant, it is also historical and conditioned by apprehension and choice in time, so that each element of the structure admits of evil. There are particular evils which cause harm, suffering, and destruction of particular goods, but so too "can there be a scheme or recurrence working" which "keeps evils recurring," in which evil can break apart the good of order in as "many ways as there are aspects of the good of order."[29] So, also, does evil negate aesthetic, ethical, and religious value through ugliness, incomprehensibility, alienation, secularism, nihilism, or superficiality, all of which are "a loss of order *within* man."[30] Consequently, while structurally invariant, the human good progresses or declines in history because of human apprehension and action, with three differentials of that movement: intellectual development (progress), sin (decline), and redemption.

Intellectual development exhibits two modes corresponding to Lonergan's distinction between the levels of intelligence and judgment, with *civilization* corresponding to intelligence and *culture* corresponding to judgment. Civilizational development operates in a mode similar

27. Lonergan, *Method*, 31–32.

28. Lonergan, *Topics in Education*, 34–35.

29. Ibid., 43–44.

30. Ibid., 44–48, at 46.

to intelligence, for from bright ideas comes action and altered situations demanding further actions: "The process functions as a wheel: situation, insight, counsel, policy, common consent, action, new situation, new insight, new counsel, new policy and so on."[31] Of course, given this developmental process, intelligence can very likely improve situations, and improved situations allow more intelligence, and so on:

> . . . this process of new ideas can spread through the whole good of order. You start changing the situation at one point, but that change in the situation will involve repercussions all through the good of order. New ideas will start popping up everywhere. There will result augmented well-being, and it affects each of the aspects of the human good: the flow of particular goods becomes more frequent, more instance, more varied; . . . new types of goods are provided; the society enjoys democracy and more education; . . . there is status for all, because everything is running smoothly; . . . there are happy personal relations, a development in taste, in aesthetic value and its appreciation, and in ethics, in the autonomy of the subject; finally, there is more time for people to attend to their own perfection in religion.[32]

In other words, all things being equal, unfettered intelligence makes things better, and better, and better, and the human good develops and progresses with no real limit since intelligence itself is unlimited, it "has no fixed frontiers," and can move the situation away from those evils negating the good. Civilizational progress is possible so long as the disinterested desire to know is not impaired or hindered and everyone is attentive, intelligent, reasonable, and responsible.

Just as civilization stems from the account of intelligence, culture stems from judgment, or reflective insight. As civilization develops, there arises the possibility for a new "apprehension of the structural invariants" of the human good, since the "mere fact of the advance of civilizational order . . . involves some sort of new incarnation, new realization, of the structural invariants."[33] Civilizational order results in new possibilities within the invariant structures of the human good—more or new particular goods, new schemes of recurrence and order, new articulations of value, but still particular goods, the good of order and value—the invariants are always operative, and thus rarely noticed or apprehended

31. Ibid., 50.
32. Ibid., 51.
33. Ibid., 55.

except obliquely. Cultural progress, on the other hand, is "progress in the apprehension of the structural invariants," from the heavy lifting of archaic symbolic images of the good to the nuanced differentiation of contemporary hermeneutical consciousness, bringing with progress not only a sophisticated apprehension of the human good but also a refinement and differentiation of the modes of human consciousness itself.[34] Cultural progress, then, is a development of the polymorphic consciousness in its apprehension of the human good in history.

Now, if humans were purely intelligent and entirely obedient to the demands of intelligence progress would ensue. But as intellectual development was the first differential, sin is the second, with decline a real possibility. Having a sophisticated account of why humans are not static substances, Lonergan gives sin its due.[35] Not merely a religious category, he indicates the understanding of sin in the thought of Marx and Nietzsche, for example, before distinguishing sin as crime, social process and aberration. Crime can be dealt with briefly, for as crime, sin is "a statistical phenomenon," and each "annual crop of infants is a potential invasion of barbarians." [36] It just simply is the case that some persons will fall prey to passion, moral failings, bad will, ignorance, and commit crimes, often as related to desires for particular goods.

More serious is sin as a differential of civilizational order. While civilization could develop in a steady advance of intelligent progress, this is not guaranteed, as indicated by earlier explanations of scotosis and bias; civilization does not "develop in the glorious fashion" possible for purely intelligent beings.[37] Instead, the good of order often skews in favor of the powerful, rich, majority, or dominant minority, with an unhealthy division into classes and resulting resentments and prejudices. Possible contributions from intelligent members of "lower" classes are overlooked and ignored, and "developments become lopsided, curtailed," creativity impaired and given fewer chances to circle into the process of progress.[38] In the face of the irrational situation, some retire into the ivory tower of private or collective isolation, detaching themselves from the situation, thus unable to contribute to change, while others attempt a revival of

34. Ibid., 58.
35. Ibid., 82–84.
36. Ibid., 59.
37. Ibid., 60.
38. Ibid.

previous systems—the ancient virtues—which are no longer possible or relevant to the current milieu. Others launch into utopian dreams, others fall into messianic hopes for technological solutions to problems of value, and the situation becomes absurd, with decline quite probable:

> ... the flight from understanding blocks the insights that concrete situations demand. There follow unintelligent policies and inept courses of action. The situation deteriorates to demand still further insights, and as they are blocked, policies become more unintelligent and action more inept. What is worse, the deteriorating situation seems to provide the uncritical, biased mind with factual evidence in which the bias is claimed to be verified. So in ever increasing measure intelligence comes to be regarded as irrelevant to practical living. Human activity settles down to a decadent routine and initiative becomes the privilege of violence.[39]

In addition to the failure of intelligence on the civilizational level, there is "the evil that is opposite to cultural development, to development on the reflective level ... to development in the apprehension of the invariants of the human good."[40] Like the human good itself, human consciousness is factical, historical, and dynamic—it is *not* settled or fixed once and for all. Not only is consciousness free to direct itself to what pleases the subject (their loves), but it dwells in social history, and *Zeitgeist* can be an aberration: "As aberrant consciousness heads to neurosis and psychosis, similarly aberrant history heads to cataclysm."[41] Aberration, which Lonergan's defines as "Sorge as functionally conflicting with pure desire to know," is a blocking off of *concern*, a denial of the exigencies of the human, a closing "of the higher aspirations of the human spirit and the human heart."[42] Aberration, thus, is a failure of love, especially the love of fully apprehending what is true, right, and good.

Rejections and blockings of intelligence and judgment results in decline, of either the shorter or longer cycles. Shorter cycles tend to be caused by group bias, especially through the neglect and oversight of beneficial ideas proposed by non-dominant groups. As troublesome as this is, Lonergan reserves particular concern for general bias and its

39. Lonergan, *Insight*, 8.
40. Ibid., 62.
41. Ibid., 63.
42. Ibid.

trajectory towards the longer cycle of decline.[43] In general bias, common sense practicality impairs the disinterested desire to know by limiting the concern of intelligence to the immediately practical, in a way distorting the capacity of intelligence's freedom to attain insight. Common sense concerns things as they relate to us and our concerns; as such, common sense is "unequal to the task of thinking on the level of history," the level in which the human good, as dynamic, is apprehended and developed, and so is ineffective in "realizing ideas, however appropriate and reasonable, that suppose a long view or that set up a higher integration or that involve the solution of intricate and disputed issues."[44] Not only can common sense not rise to the level of higher integration, but it can twist intelligence so that unless ideas have some obvious and immediate payoff they are ignored and thought nugatory, thus disregarded.

As biased practical intelligence disregards ideas which could inform good policies and actions, it also tends to result not merely in the failure to attain good results but also in furthering worsening conditions, for "[c]orrupt minds have a flair for picking the mistaken solution and insisting that it alone is intelligent. . . . A civilization in decline digs its own grave with a relentless consistency."[45] First, the social situation worsens, with conflicts between individuals and groups turning into incoherencies between schemes of recurrence, some atrophying and others growing "like tumors . . . penetrated with anomalies."[46] Second, the detached intelligence is disregarded, thought useless, disreputable: "Culture retreats into an ivory tower. Religion becomes an inward affair of the heart. Philosophy glitters like a gem with endless facets and no practical purpose."[47] Third, now irrelevant, the desire to know gives in to a "minor surrender," and intelligence capitulates to the daily business of life, perhaps offering a brief respite in moments of leisure, but still controlled to the tune of immediate practicality. There can also be a major surrender when intelligence and its precepts are reduced to the sort of objectivity proper only to animal knowing, to a kind of positivism, and intelligence instrumentalized into a mere tool of studying the data and claiming as knowable and real only that which is generalizable from

43. Ibid., 251–61.
44. Ibid., 253.
45. Lonergan, *Method*, 55.
46. Lonergan, *Insight*, 254.
47. Ibid.

the data. This sort of reductionistic scientism causes a "new culture, a new religion, a new philosophy," one which is "empirical, scientific, realistic."[48] And despite all the possible advances in knowledge which this hard-headed study might allow, its refusal to allow the exigencies of subjectivity means that this culture is, in the end, bereft of the ability to distinguish progress from the mere demands of practicality, and intelligence cedes its norms to that of bias, which is destructive of intelligence and all but guarantees that the most fruitful of ideas and policies will be neglected and shunted aside in favor of the superficially expedient, whatever its costs. Further, in so damaging intelligence, the culture made possible by the disinterested desire to know is replaced with a new culture, a new and somewhat perverted apprehension of the good, one beneath human dignity. Genuinely wicked and reprehensible systems can result, both hard and soft totalitarianisms in which freedom is betrayed for bread, dignity for the soft comforts and relishes of the indulgent, even willing to kill, maim, farm, cannibalize, and destroy all and everyone in the name of immanent immediacy.

Cosmopolis and Reversing Decline

So, there is progress, and there is decline. Progress occurs when humans are free to follow the norms of subjectivity and live in keeping with the self-correcting process of our conscious operations. In principle, progress can be ongoing, resulting in better and better developments at all levels of value. However, there is also decline, and its principle is bias:

> Man's intelligence, reasonableness, and willingness (1) proceed from a detached, disinterested, unrestricted desire to know, (2) are potentialities in process of development . . . stand in opposition and tension with sensitive and intersubjective attachment, interest . . . suffer from that tension a cumulative bias that increasingly distorts immanent development. . . . The problem is radical, for it a problem in the very dynamic structure of cognitional, volitional, and social activity. It is not a question of error on this or that general or particular issue. It is a question of orientation, approach, procedure, method.[49]

It is important to note the language of *orientation*. Decline is not primarily caused by error or mistaken policy but by an inauthentic orientation.

48. Ibid., 255.
49. Ibid., 655.

This occurs in the domain of meaning, horizon, stance, *Sorge*, *molestia*, *tentatio*, engagement, desire—within *love*. Decline occurs when loves are distorted and inadequate in their basic directedness or orientation, and when the horizons in which we operate and move are restricted, closed, scotistic, aberrant—when they are biased. Decline occurs when our basic stance towards the world is not the authentic stance of the desire to know grounded by our operations in their cumulative, self-corrective, developmental, and progressive structure, but when the underlying and basic loves driving the same structure are disordered and aberrant. Decline is a failure of love.

The solution to decline is consequently a change of basic and fundamental loves, of horizon, orientation, engagement, directedness, stance, *Sorge*, *curare*—each of the thinkers examined in this text use varying language—but the various expressions disclose that any solution will be a solution of love, a "higher integration of human loving . . . a further manifestation of finality, of the upwardly but indeterminately directed dynamism."[50]

For Lonergan, this higher integration occurs in the world of meaning, in the domain of *culture*, the human "capacity to ask, to reflect, to reach an answer that at once satisfies his intelligence and speaks to his heart."[51] Culture is a horizon of meaning, a stance of engagement towards the world, a pre-judgment in which the world appears, and a re-ordering of horizons of love will be a reordering of pre-judgments of what counts as significant and insignificant, as worth being concerned about. Humans move from the infant's world of immediacy to the world mediated by meaning, which is not within immediate experience or even within cumulative human experience but rather within what is conceived of an intelligible, real, and knowable.[52] Meaning is not static or settled however, and the devices, symbols, and intellectual tools serving as the controls of meaning "mark off the great epochs in human history."[53] Classical culture controlled meaning through logic, a science of necessary and universal causes, and a study of human nature, whereas modern culture did so through method, probability, and interiority. In either instance, culture is the means by which historical consciousness

50. Ibid., 655–56.

51. Ibid., 261.

52. Lonergan, *Collection*, 232–33.

53. Ibid., 235.

differentiations, symbolizes, and controls what counts as meaningful, possible, or significant, and so Lonergan thinks that if "men are to meet the challenge set by major decline and its longer cycle, it will be through their culture that they do so."[54]

A turn to culture is not a panacea for decline, however, as aberration makes even culture irrational and a contributing factor to decline, especially when culture capitulates to general bias, in which case "culture renounces its one essential function, and by that renunciation condemns practicality to ruin."[55] In the longer cycle of decline, apprehension of the invariant structure of the good is distorted, and expressions of value and policy begin more and more to indiscriminately "close upon a closer harmony with the fact of the social surd . . . culture ceases to be an independent factor that passes a detached yet effective judgment upon capital formation and technology, upon economy and polity. To justify its existence, it ha[s] to become more and more practical, more and more a . . . tool that served palpably useful ends."[56] What is needed to overcome decline, therefore, is a sound cultural community:

> a cosmopolis that is neither class nor state, that stands above all their claims, that cuts them down to size, that is founded on the native detachment and disinterestedness of every intelligence, that commands man's first allegiance, that implements itself primarily through that allegiance, that is too universal to be bribed, too impalpable to be forced, too effective to be ignored.[57]

Lonergan follows with four aspects of cosmopolis. First, it is not an institution of force or governance, not some superstate or world power, for it is above governance and the incidental concerns of this or that problem; its "business is to prevent practicality from being shortsightedly practical and so destroying itself."[58] Secondly, general bias creates a vicious circle whereby good ideas and policies are rendered inoperative because no one will act on them because since the ideas are out-of-step with their desires, and because no one acts on the ideas there is no empirical evidence that they will work, reinforcing the suspicion. The task of cosmopolis is to "make operative the timely and fruitful ideas

54. Ibid., 261.
55. Ibid., 262.
56. Ibid.
57. Ibid., 263.
58. Ibid., 264.

that otherwise are inoperative," which it does by providing witness to the fruitful ideas of intelligence without resorting to force.[59] Thirdly, as reversing general bias and the longer pattern of decline, cosmopolis does not concern itself with condemning and reversing individual or group bias—it is not a busybody attempting to root out every vice and correct every ill. However, when dominant groups (group bias) attempt to rationalize their sins by turning sins into "universal principles," or when a newly dominant group uses myth to demonize or dehumanize the previous elite, then cosmopolis acts to "prevent the formation of the screening memories," the ideologies, the *agitprop*, and the second realities that make truth a captive and force all to live lies.[60] Fourthly, just as cosmopolis hopes to protect the future against rationalization and myth, so it critiques history and the rationalizations and myth carried along to infect the present.

In the early chapters, our description of Lonergan's cognitional theory articulated the invariant, dynamic structure of human knowing and acting. Driven by the disinterested desire to know, humans move from experience, to understanding, to judgment, to choice. Further, driven by the same desire, humans can know themselves in the referentially consistent, and performatively irrefutable method of self-appropriation whereby they experience themselves experiencing, understanding, judging and choosing; understanding what it is to experience, understand, judge, and choose; judging that they are knowers and agents who experience, understanding, judge, and choose; and choosing to live in keeping with the norms of experiencing, understanding, judging, and choosing.[61] Choosing the structure is more than simply judging that it is correct, it is "deciding to operate in accord with the norms immanent" in the operations—with those norms summarized in the precepts "Be attentive! Be intelligent! Be reasonable! Be responsible!"—this is an existential choice, a *decision to live in keeping with the norms of love as they operate within human subjectivity.*

Such a life is authenticity, the ongoing, free activity of constituting the self we are and will be. Given our factical, temporal reality, authenticity is an activity, "not a content per se; rather it is an ongoing

---

59. Ibid.

60. Ibid., 265. For powerful analysis, see Milosz, *Captive Mind*, or Voegelin, *History of the Race Idea*.

61. Ibid., 343–71; *Method*, 3–25.

activity of conversion [intellectual, moral, and religious], the fullness of self-transcendence," the "continuous dialectic between development and decline."[62] Previous chapters explained conversion in its three types, but important here is the linking of authenticity, conversion, and self-transcendence. The higher integration of cosmopolis, the cultural community of reversing decline, requires transcendence, which means a "going beyond."[63] Insofar as one is capable of following the transcendental precepts, the dynamism of consciousness allows consciousness itself to serve as an immanent source of transcendence, moving us beyond our own interests and satisfactions—beyond even bias: "By experience we attend to the other; by understanding we gradually construct our world; by judgment we discern its independence of ourselves; by deliberative and responsible freedom we move beyond merely self-regarding norms and make ourselves moral beings."[64] This is the process of development from below upward, where the dynamism of intellect—the love of the real—extends further to include choice and action (the love of the good), driving humans forward beyond themselves and their narrow interests towards what *really* is true and *really* is good. Humans can move from within their own subjectivity towards progress and the reversal of decline, with love operating as an immanent norm manifested as the detached, disinterested desire to know."[65]

The Reign of Sin

Cosmopolis is difficult, but it has allies in common sense, which "tends to be profoundly sane," as well as dialectical analysis' exposure of "resistance to enlightenment."[66] Still, however capable we are of development from below upwards, common sense is not enough, for the problem indicated in this and previous chapters is that while sustained, continual, and self-correcting development (progress) requires the unimpaired exigencies of human intelligence and the personal and collective will do what is intelligent and reasonable, there is *sin*, and thus no sustained development. The problem, Lonergan suggests, "is radical, for it is a

62. Braman, *Meaning and Authenticity*, 58–59.
63. Lonergan, *Insight*, 658.
64. Quoted in Lawrence, "Lonergan and Aquinas," 449.
65. Lonergan, *Insight*, 659–62.
66. Ibid., 267.

problem in the very dynamic structure of cognitional, volitional, and social activity," and it is not a question merely of mistake or error, but "a question of orientation," or care, hindering "every use of the dynamic structure."[67] The problem is permanent, evil is a fact, and neither alterations of the social situation, or a "correct philosophy, ethics, or human science," or a new system of power will effect much, for the solution "has to be a still higher integration of human living," which demands a supernatural solution, redemption.[68] If "the need of some cosmopolis makes manifest the inadequacy of common sense to deal with [bias], on a deeper level it makes manifest the inadequacy of man."[69]

While Lonergan rightly holds to a notion of human development where the operator of progress is human consciousness, he knows that in addition to the love of insight and truth, there can be "a love of darkness," governed by bias.[70] This is more than an intellectual failure, however, for "[B]ad will is not merely the inconsistency of rational self-consciousness; it is also sin against God. The hopeless tangle of the social surd, of the impotence of common sense, of the endlessly multiplied philosophies, is not merely a *cul-de-sac* for human progress; it also is a reign of sin, a despotism of darkness; and men are its slaves."[71] When love is fundamentally imprisoned, love cannot free itself.

In *Topics in Education*, Lonergan suggests that given "grave sin," it is impossible without grace to avoid moral impotence as well as distorted cultural systems: "The moral impotence in man creates in man a demand for false philosophies . . . for a high-level rationalization, just as it created a demand for degrading myths in ancient times."[72] Consequently, neither the philosopher nor the bard provide true philosophies or symbols of the good life, but rather captivity to darkness, irrationality, distortion, ideology, and a dimming of heart and mind into systems of meaning demonic in their incoherence. This moral cataclysm is overcome only through conversion, through redemption, for what is needed "is a leap—not a leap beyond reason . . . but a leap from unreason, from the unreasonableness of sin, to reason," but such a leap

67. Lonergan, *Insight*, 653.

68. Ibid., 654–55.

69. Ibid., 712.

70. Ibid., 214.

71. Ibid., 714.

72. Lonergan, *Topics in Education*, 64.

to reason is not merely "a matter of repeating, pronouncing, affirming, agreeing with the propositions that are true," but real and thorough apprehension of reality—this is "something existential."[73] The cultural solution of cosmopolis, this enormous achievement of the human spirit, is ultimately *not* the solution to the problem of evil, taking us into the realm of conversion, redemption, and the love of God.

The Love of God Poured into Human Hearts

Redemption, the third differential of the human good in history, is a "break with the past, the dead hand of the past, its institutions . . . resentments and hatreds. . . . "[74] The various religions and symbolic systems provide distinct accounts of redemption's meaning and practices, with cultic symbols, rites, and mediators. However, for the Christian, redemption comes "in Christ Jesus," who did not do as was expected and transform the world by destroying the unjust and inaugurating prosperity for his people; instead, redemption in Christ "does not change the fundamental fact that sin continues to head for suffering and death" although that evil is given "new significance" in the crucifixion and resurrection, baptism and Eucharist.[75] For Lonergan, *faith* is the answer to the problem of sin, both for the next life and for the crimes, social disorders, and aberrations of this life, for faith puts false idols and ideologies in their place, restores the truth of reality as meaningful, as ultimate, and with truth re-established liberates intelligence from the aberrations of cultural decline. So liberated, faith allows also *hope* for social process, unblocking creativity and intelligence from the effects of sin and allowing the human subject—now themselves freed from captivity and blindness—to free the captives and loose the blind around them through insight, and counsel, and policy, and action of good, and sustained intelligence in history. Against the perpetuating cycle of crime and violence, there is *love* of enemies and the acceptance of suffering.[76]

In previous chapters, we explained Lonergan's account of how religious conversion grounds both moral and religious conversion, for captivity to the reign of sin means that without religious conversion we

73. Ibid.
74. Ibid., 65.
75. Ibid., 66–67.
76. Ibid., 67.

remain prisoners and captives in the darkness, ineffective against decline. And we've explained how religious conversion allows for affective development and authenticity. There is no need to reiterate all those arguments, but it is vital to emphasize how religious conversion is primarily about *love* and the reorientation of horizons. For Lonergan, we achieve "authenticity in self-transcendence," and we do not live "locked up in oneself" but in a horizon of disclosure, open to the world in attention, understanding, judging, and choosing.[77] However, the authenticity of self-transcendence is merely a capacity which "becomes an actuality when one falls in love. Then one's being becomes being-in-love."[78] As one's mode of being, it "lasts, it takes over," and from the horizon of love, from this fundamental state of being (*Sorge*) "flow one's desires and fears, one's joys and sorrow, one's discernment of values, one's decisions and deeds."[79]

Love takes various forms, but being in love with God is the terminus and "basic fulfillment of our conscious intentionality," as the love of God floods "our hearts through the Holy Spirit given to us (Rom. 5, 5)."[80] This love is unrestricted, without limits or conditions, and is the fulfillment of the capacity for self-transcendence. Unlike development from below, it "is not the product of our knowledge and choice . . . it dismantles and abolishes the horizon in which our knowing and choosing went on and sets up a new horizon in which the love of God will transvalue our values and the eyes of that love will transform our knowing."[81] This conversion is a gift of God, and, importantly, is a reorientation on the scale of *value*, of what is loved and desired and chosen prior to a change of understanding or judgment of fact—it most definitely *does not* begin with worldview analysis, although it might end there.

Love allows for faith, and in the eyes of faith value enlarges. Without faith, the human good is the limit of value, but with faith the originating value "is divine light and love" and "the human good becomes absorbed in an all-encompassing good," which goes far beyond narrow individual interest, or group interest, or even the all-consuming desire to make things better in general bias, for God's love overcomes even death. Faith

77. Lonergan, *Method*, 104.

78. Ibid., 105.

79. Ibid.

80. Ibid.

81. Ibid., 106.

in love allows progress, for it meets "the challenge of human decline," and overcomes "inattention, oversights, irrationality, irresponsibility."[82] And love does all of this in keeping with human subjectivity, for while love can shatter horizons and reorder feelings, love transforms or converts orientations and overcomes the reign of sin and decline by allowing for genuine subjectivity. It does not turn us into something other than humans but allows the human spirit to be fulfilled in itself and in its capacities for progress, both individually and in collaboration with others. Being-in-love as a gift of God allows humans to be and do as they should be and do, and beyond the limits of development from below upwards. The wholeness and order to follow allows for a radical decentering of the self, a "displacement of the subject" such that concern and love for the other person, and even for the whole universe, outstrips self-satisfaction, and allows the human to cooperate with God and others "to sustain and realize the order of the universe."[83]

Human achievement from below allows for cosmopolis to be grasped as a heuristic ideal, but in the end authenticity is a matter of conversion, an ongoing activity of self-transcendence allowing the higher integration cosmopolis aims for; but unless one's "whole world is changed and reoriented around the mystery of absolute love," the problem of evil and decline is without effective solution. Cosmopolis as a cultural community is made possible by authenticity, authenticity is self-transcendence, and self-transcendence is, in the end, being-in-love. The culmination of human living, and of the imperatives or precepts that noetic exegesis discovers, is love: what it means to "Be attentive, Be intelligent, Be reasonable, Be responsible" as a true human being, one who is transformed by God, is to be-in-love.

CONCLUSION

We certainly do not claim that this chapter solves the various issues of contemporary cosmopolitan thought, nor answers its detractors, for those issues are not identical with the cosmopolis of Lonergan's understanding. Yet the topics are not entirely dissimilar, for cosmopolitan thought attempts to go beyond the natural affections of family and clan, beyond the passions of state and nation to form a concern (and

82. Ibid., 117.
83. Braman, *Meaning and Authenticity*, 69–70.

consequent institutions and policies) exhibiting solidarity for the development, dignity, justice, and flourishing of all; for the cosmopolitan, everyone is a neighbor and thus owed love. And yet bias and decline render that problematic, unlikely even, if not for self-transcendence, but the reign of sin makes transcendence unlikely.

In his lucid analysis, Joshua Yates explains the "problem of the good world," or "the cosmopolitan predicament," in a way revealing how relevant Lonergan is to cosmopolitanism, even when cosmopolis goes far beyond cosmopolitanism.[84] As Yates summarizes the situation, the current revival of cosmopolitanism entails the way we envision or map the world, and so is an "imagination," an "outlook", a "conceptual reconfiguration" in "*how humans apprehend the world.*" [85] The changing apprehension includes an impact "on consciousness itself," with the impact described as "reflexivity," self-aware of its contingency and placement in history and heritage. Our "orientation to the world grows over more critically reflexive, yet . . . more universalist, interventionist, and prescriptive at the same time."[86] We envision or imagine the world as one, with "the ethical aspirations of universal brotherhood and the respect for the fundamental dignity of all humans no longer . . . figurative and abstract," although the realities of globalization render such aspirations problematic.[87] We are now asked to see our commitments differently, extending even to those whom we do not know and cannot quite understand how our agency effects, "a dramatic transformation in world pictures."[88]

Cosmopolitanism would seem to be a shift in consciousness, a change in how contemporaries apprehend world order and relations, including, but not limited to, the good of order. It thus would appear to be what Lonergan would call a *cultural* development, a way of apprehending the structure of the good, or as Yates expresses:

> . . . the new cosmopolitanism exhorts us to pay heed to how we humans apprehend our world The symbolic importance of the revival of cosmopolitanism calls us to attend to the full range of the empirical and moral challenges or our changing world pic-

84. Yates, "Mapping the Good World," 25.

85. Ibid.,10–11.

86. Ibid., 17.

87. Ibid., 26.

88. Ibid.

ture . . . living amid the tensions generated by reinvigorated ethical and political aspirations for a better, more humane, and just world and repeated confrontation with the intractable disorders, dislocations, and failures wrought by these very same forces. As a result, human beings are undergoing a difficult and uncertain period, not only of economic and political reordering, but of profound moral reorientation.[89]

So while the cultural development calls for a new apprehension of the good, this very apprehension reveals the results of the reign of sin and the various differences, conflicts, sufferings, poverty, injustices, individual biases, group biases, general biases, and aberrations. A cultural shift without a concomitant shift of self-transcendence may provide an ideal but not the freedom to attain the ideal.

Lonergan's cosmopolis accomplishes several tasks. First, linking the human good and education closely with bias and sin. Second, providing an account of the reversal of decline rooted in the immanent operations of consciousness, thus linking human subjectivity and its intentional structures to teleology and human achievement, with cosmopolis serving as a heuristic for a certain kind of culture or orientation of love. Third, frankly acknowledging the limits of achievement and the necessity of redemption as the condition of possibility of self-transcendence, authenticity, and the reversal of decline. Fourth, in a contemporary context in which the goal of global citizenship is strong, Lonergan provides a structural and cultural back-story to that ideal—and its predicaments—in the invariant structures of consciousness as well as the differentials of human history which spur or impede cosmopolitan hopes.

With respect to those hopes, universities mirror the concerns and horizons of their time; consequently, for the current university, questions of citizenship are unavoidable, reflecting the reality of globalization and increased integration of the world. No longer can universities prepare graduates for the "nation's service," but rather as citizens of the world, as cosmopolitans.[90] Christian universities follow suit, although Christian education has always resided in something of a tension with respect to citizenship, for Christians reside as dual citizens of the City of God and the City of Man, with absolute allegiances to the first city and its transcultural reality—neither Jew nor Greek—and merely relative

89. Ibid., 27.
90. Wilson, "Princeton in the Nation's Service."

duties to the second.[91] Consequently, the Christian university, like its secular counterparts, has good reason to consider itself in global rather than merely national context, although the Christian university in its catholicity has its own peculiar reasons to do so.

One particularly compelling reason for Christian universities to take cosmopolitanism seriously is its close linkage to solidarity and justice. Notions of what is meant by the "good citizen" in distinction to the "good person" are as old, if not older, than *Antigone*, and the cosmopolitan has always thought of themselves as linked in solidarity to all, regardless of tribe, religion, or nation, thus owing every person what is due to his or her common humanity.[92] Christian education is inadequate unless committed to value, what Nicholas Wolterstorff, a powerful and influential advocate for a Reformed vision, terms "shalom": "Can the Christian college do anything else than guide its endeavors by this vision of shalom? If God's call to all humanity is to be liberators and developers, celebrators and mourners; and if to that call of God the church of Jesus Christ replies with a resonant yes, then will not the Christian college have to find its place within this great commission?"[93]

Still, it is easy to view such visions as utopian, as a hope from nowhere of a place which does not, cannot exist, where aspirations are thought possible by fiat, in deep ignorance of the human condition in its finitude, fallibility, and wickedness.[94] If we are to have a coherent vision of cosmopolitanism and shalom, it would need to be one in keeping with the ways of love, and thus a culmination of the values of a fully converted subject loved by, and in love with, God. But a subject of facticity, operating in history, community, embodiment, and limits of our created order.

91. Manent, *Intellectual History of Liberalism*, 3–9; Manent, *City of Man*; Hays, *Moral Vision of the New Testament*, 407–43.

92. Delanty, *Cosmopolitan Imagination*, 89–110.

93. Wolterstorff, *Educating for Shalom*, 23. See also Plantinga, *Engaging God's World*, 20; Pally, *New Evangelicals*; Wolterstorff, *Justice*.

94. McPartland, *Lonergan and the Philosophy of Historical Existence*, 37–50.

CONCLUSION

An Education for Our Time

We view this text as contributing to the literature on Christian higher education, pulling in the same direction as others attempting to go beyond pedagogies captured by an anthropology of the thinking thing. We are primarily lovers, not thinkers, and since every pedagogy presupposes its anthropology, getting the anthropology right is a matter of priority. Consequently, we zeroed in on a claim made by James Smith that a study of intentionality reveals something of importance about love, and also for education. The vast majority of the text is a study of intentionality, of love, both in a creative retrieval of historical sources and in conversation with more contemporary thinkers. Our account of subjectivity, does, we think, offer something of value to the conversation, independent of its implications for education, although more work remains to be done on those implications, not only by us but by others involved in the conversation. In this conclusion we provide only some basic principles from which to do more work, with those principles grounded deeply in our account of love. First, a bit of summary.

Without love there is no knowledge or action, for knowledge precedes and follows upon our intentional operations. We exist in a world opened to us by care, *cura*, *Sorge*, and we can pivot attention to our loves in a noetic exegesis or intentionality analysis disclosing how it is that we operate consciously. Such pivoting is not some sort of inner look or super-introspection through the mind's privileged access to itself but an advertence to the very operations by which we know and act—we experience, understand, judge, and choose our experiencing, understanding, judging and choosing. This self-appropriation reveals the invariant structures of human subjectivity and reveals what we do, who we are, and how we do what we do, as well as revealing the norms of subjectivity.

The condition of subjectivity is love, for without the dynamic desire to know and choose the real the operations never get moving, never operate, and we would not be able to engage either the world or ourselves.

While the Western tradition sometimes fails in its understanding of subjectivity, some thinkers stand out, even when limited by their own historical moment and the language available to them. A creative retrieval of Plato, Augustine, and Aquinas, especially when read with questions of intentionality in the foreground, reveals an anthropology not beholden to static models of human nature and its apparatus of essence, soul, and faculty. Human nature can be considered on the model of the concrete, existing subject, which is more adequate to how we actually are in the world; these thinkers, and others such as Heidegger, Taylor, and Lonergan, allow for a an account which is critically grounded, concrete, normative, and known through adverting to our own selves.

Turning to the subject, moreover, need not be a turn to the solipsistic self of Descartes trapped behind the veil of ideas, for there is no subject/object split to overcome in a genuine account of subjectivity, especially if one grasps the primacy of love. The world, its entities and persons, are not divorced from our concerns and engaged involvements, and while there are no ahistorical, disembodied, punctual, or non-perspectival selves, there is also no entrapment in the secret recesses of inner space. Rather, the turn is to a real person, with a heritage, a history, a society, and a horizon of meaning largely given by that self's thrownness. This factical self is always already in a world of interest and concern, a world always involving socially shared meanings and projects (understandings), and without that facticity the self would be nothing.

Concrete human subjects are always already involved, they are being-there in the world, always engaged in certain stances and projects, certain ways of being interested or concerned, and so occupy a "world space" of value, evaluations, and moral structure. We are never not in a world of values and engagement, and the turn to the subject always discovers a decentered subject of self-transcendence. Even to experience data is to exist beyond the confines of the mind and engagement with the world in our interpretations, and directedness; the world "means" because we care, and are condemned always to care, even if that care is dynamic and changing. The turn to subjectivity, then, and its noetic exegesis, is simultaneously a hermeneutics of facticity.

Leaving Descartes' ghost behind, and the pedagogies chained to that ghost, the real question concerns the quality of the loves one has, whether the loves and the self who loves are authentic or inauthentic. There are good reasons to pause before embracing authenticity as a category, however, especially since the avenue of the metaphysics of the soul is inadequate. Consequently, the teleology of the proper functioning soul, so prevalent in certain schools of thought, is not available to noetic exegesis—those categories would simply be out of place. Authenticity, therefore, if it is to be critically grounded and normative rather than merely narcissistic, requires an account of normativity.

Intentionality analysis reveals more than operations, for the method reveals not just an invariant structure of consciousness but also an invariant structure of the human good. In an ordered cosmos, the natural exigencies of intentionality are themselves norms, for the dynamic and disinterested desire for self-transcendence is normative. If subjects followed the norms of subjectivity—Be attentive! Be intelligent! Be reasonable! Be responsible!—they would seek and attain true value in its many forms (vital, social, cultural, moral, religious). Further, self-transcending authenticity would result in progress and human achievement for individuals, civilizations, and cultures.

While the universe is ordered, the reign of sin caused by and causing bias interferes and distorts individuals, civilizations, and cultures. Shorter and longer patterns of decline result, with bad choices, bad policy, and bad actions tending towards entropy, chaos, stupidity, injustice, greed, and violence, in both personal and systemic forms. As tempting as it is to respond to decline with practicality, an improper commitment to practicality is itself a bias interfering with intelligence, and biased minds and systems tend to make even worse choices in their relentless drive into decline.

Decline is reversed with a cultural shift, with cosmopolis, a renewed communal apprehension of genuine value governed by the intelligent, reasonable, and responsible norms of subjectivity. Yet, cosmopolis is impotent to respond to evil, for sin cannot be overcome or reversed by human achievement, and a supernatural answer—grace, redemption—is needed.

Just as subjectivity is concrete, sin and grace are not abstract pieces to move about in the puzzle of theory. A hermeneutics of facticity allows sin and grace to be grasped in their concrete, historical, embodied real-

ity, as sin and grace operate within the structures of human consciousness, with grace affecting the self-transcendence of intellectual, moral,
and religious conversion.

Intellectual conversion overcomes the limits of corporeal thinking
and grasps that the real is not merely what can be seen and that objectivity is not reducible to a close look. Moral conversion moves the subject
beyond mere self-interest and the satisfaction of particular desires, and
turns loves toward genuine value. Religious conversion grounds the other conversions and is the dynamic state of being-in-love, a state which
shatters the distortions of bias and its limited, skewed horizons and
concerns, remakes desires, questions, values, affectivity, skills, insights,
judgments—it remakes the world of meaning and allows for genuine
subjectivity, for authentic human existence, and for civilizational and
cultural progress—religious conversion allows cosmopolis.

The dynamic state of being-in-love is a gift of God and occurs when
the love of God is poured into our hearts by the Holy Spirit, when human lives becomes shaped by the life of God. In love, we become friends
with God, each other, the world, and our own selves. God's love makes
us in love with everything, makes us what we are to be, and what we are
for. And all manner of things are made well.

PRINCIPLES FOR A TIMELY EDUCATION

Any education fit for humans accords with the structure of human subjectivity. One of our tasks has been to correct a flawed philosophical
anthropology behind so much thinking about education, namely, that
we are primarily thinking things and that education is primarily about
knowledge, ideas, and worldviews. Now, certainly there can be no coherent opposition to an interest in the creation and dissemination of
knowledge in its various forms, or an interest in understanding how
ideals and values hang together in worldviews, and we offer no such
opposition; nor do we suggest an education in sentimentality. But we
suggest the anthropology sketched in this text is correct, and that an
anthropology of love is the best guide for a philosophy of education.
As mentioned previously, we do not here offer an ideal curriculum or
vision of the practices, governance, or content of a university education,
but briefly offer four guiding principles stemming from our account of
subjectivity.

Principle One: An Education for Polymorphism

Good education accords with the structures of subjectivity and aids appropriation of those structures. Lonergan's project is not something to be grasped theoretically, as a series of propositions for which other propositions are marshaled as support, but is instead a kind of critical existentialism whereby the evidence for the account is our own ability to grasp our performance. Self-appropriation, or noetic exegesis, cannot occur in the abstract; reading about appropriation does not count as evidence. In fact, our account claims to be (1) self-referentially consistent and (2) resistant to radical revision since it demonstrates itself through the same operations it proposes—one experiences, understands, judges, and chooses what it is to experience, understand, judge, and choose—and any denial of our account utilizes experience, understanding, judgment and choices in the denial, thus performatively demonstrating the truth of the account.

To understand the performance of one's intellect is no easy accomplishment, but understanding it thoroughly is to understand the full range of how humans can be in the world. As Lonergan puts it, "Thoroughly understand what it is to understand, and not only will you understand the broad lines of all there is to be understood but also you will possess a fixed base, an invariant pattern, opening upon all further developments of understanding."[1]

Understanding ourselves requires apprehending the historical nature of consciousness as well as the historical nature of meaning, which develops and alters over time and community. There may very well be an invariant structure, but there is little invariant content to be found in data, concepts, vocabulary, or meaning. Subjectivity is historical in a thoroughgoing sense, and failing to understand this is a failure to comprehend understanding. One task for education is to appreciate how meaning works in history, to understand that symbols and meanings change and develop, as do personal and social horizons, and even the modes in which consciousness operates, including those modes of care from which we engage the world. Consequently, the world changes in time.

Self-appropriation requires coming to terms with the polymorphism of consciousness, for subjectivity is diverse; humans can "be" in

---

1. Lonergan, *Insight*, 22.

the world in many different ways, and there is something to understand and value in that polymorphism, for it causes the variance and depth of our lives. Self-appropriation allows for a normative and invariant base from which to distinguish authenticity from inauthenticity, nonsense from sense, and richness from mere indulgence, but that same invariant base reveals the glorious breadth and depth and diversity of authenticity, and requires humans at home with everything human, able to dwell alongside all that is, rather than in provincial resentment of anything alien. Such an education makes space to engage all that is worth study, and that is a large space. Consequently, the best of the old and the new—not just the old or just the new—is worthwhile, and unlike older systems concerned primarily with the first and highest, the universal and the necessary, polymorphism admits that the smallest and the least, the particular and contingent are also worth consideration and care. All that is, is lovely, intelligible, worthwhile, for Christ plays in many thousands of places, lovely in them all. Of course, the range of polymorphism is enormous, unlimited, for the range of human concern is *everything thought worth engaging*. No one person can engage in all things, and so genuine education will be thoroughly collaborative, but a collaboration made intelligible by the invariant structures of subjectivity grounding the range of what is known. Concern is unlimited, but we can understand concern.

This balance between richness and foundation, invariance and diversity, is a form of hospitality, an openness to the real. Knowing the finitude and temporality of subjectivity requires a certain friendliness to polymorphism. It is, as Lonergan puts it, an education for the holding of the center:

> There is bound to be formed a solid right that is determined to live in a world that no longer exists. There is bound to be formed a scattered left, captivated by now this, now that new development, exploring now this and now that new possibility. But what will count is a perhaps not numerous center, big enough to be at home in both the old and the new, painstaking enough to work out one by one the transitions to be made, strong enough to refuse half-measures and insist on complete solutions even though it has to wait.[2]

---

2. Lonergan, *Collection*, 245.

Principle Two: An Education for Progress

We think because we love. Education according with our nature is an education in love, and while systems of thought and worldviews have their place, education is first about value, conversion, authenticity. In the introduction we claimed that education required "a reference point outside of knowledge itself, to serve as magnetic 'north' in defining liberal education's purpose," and that authentic love was true north.[3] Authenticity is not the freedom of the disengaged, free-floating self, but rather "the measure of personal authenticity for all is to be found in action, in the quality of one's choices"; the test of a good life and a good education are the same, "it is a question either of richness or of emptiness of life, and these are the direct fruits of free decisions rather than of our knowledge."[4]

No other option is possible, for we are condemned to moral meaning, and we never operate except in moral space, in evaluation, engagement, and value: "Human culture is always moral order. Human cultures are everywhere moral orders. Human persons are nearly inescapably moral agents. . . . And human institutions are inevitably morally infused configurations. . . ."[5] Consequently, education concerns the human good in its historical development—vital, social, cultural, personal, and religious values and the differentials of their development. For Lonergan, progress bears a particular relation to cultural value, those horizons of meaning and significance which avoid sinking into an irrational practicality concerned only with vital and social goods: "Cultural values do not exist without the underpinning of vital and social values, but none the less they rank higher. Not on bread alone doth man live. Over and above mere living and operating, men have to find a meaning and value in their living and operating. It is the function of culture to discover, express, validate, criticize, correct, develop, improve such meaning and value."[6]

Just as progress bears relation to cultural value, so too the university:

> A university is a reproductive organ of cultural community. Its constitutive endowment lies not on buildings or equipment, civil

3. Monan, "Value Proposition."
4. Ibid.
5. C. Smith, *Moral, Believing Animals*, 7.
6. Lonergan, *Method*, 32.

status or revenues, but in the intellectual life of its professors. Its
central function is the communication of intellectual development.... Without developed understanding ... truths become
uncomprehended formulas, moral precepts narrow down to lists
of prohibitions, and human living settles into a helpless routine ... without the power of knowledge that inspires and directs
the movement from real possibility to concrete achievement.[7]

Recall that cultural development occurs in the apprehension of the
human good, and it is cultural distortion which is largely responsible
for the longer pattern of decline whereby civilization digs its grave. An
education in cultural value, then, or a developing apprehension of genuine value, is the university's contribution to progress and the keeping of
decline at bay.

Principle Three: An Education for Cosmopolis

Progress is not inevitable, and decline is a real possibility. A temptation
exists for the university to collaborate without reservation in the general
bias of practicality, as if the university existed merely for the lower end
of the scale of values, namely the provision of vital values (particular
goods) and social values (good of order), while overlooking religious,
personal, and cultural values.[8] The challenge is less about civilizational
order than it is *cultural* development. That is, the university exists to
maintain progress and reverse decline by maintaining cosmopolis.

The "not numerous center" indicated in the first principle ought
to be particularly concerned with the real possibility of decline and its
causes in distorted culture. A primary task of the university, although
certainly not just the university, would be the formation of "a creative
minority that grasps what is going forward, understands its roots,
anticipates its consequences, and decides to resist it and to offer an
alternative."[9] Such a creative minority would be a "[c]osmopolitan intelligence ... inform[ing] an intellectual collaboration that assumes the
integrity of culture as its principal responsibility and that implements
this responsibility through a reorientation especially of the human sciences" in accord with authentic subjectivity.[10]

7. Lonergan, *Collection*, 111.

8. Doran, *Theological Foundations*, 367.

9. Ibid., 372.

10. Ibid., 373.

The university serves as a community committed to the integrity of culture, but Christian and secular varieties "exercise the same function" in that respect, for both exist for the sake of "communicating intellectual development."[11] But the secular university is somewhat less capable of doing so, for it is "caught in the ambiguities of civil and cultural development-and-decline; it may lag in consenting to aberrations but in the long run it has to yield" since all persons involved are formed by their community and its decline—sheer intelligence is no answer to the reign of sin. A culture in aberration requires cosmopolis informed by redemption.[12] To be sure, the persons involved in Christian education are not somehow free from cultural entanglement, but are

> armed against the world. The supernatural virtues of faith, hope, and charity are named theological because they orientate man to God as he is in himself. Nonetheless, they possess a profound social significance. Against the perpetuation of explosive tensions . . . there is the power of charity. . . . Against the economic determinism . . . there is the liberating power of hope. . . . Against the dialectic discernible in the . . . development-and-decline of civil and cultural communities, there is the liberation of human reason through divine faith. . . .[13]

The supernatural virtues are gifts from God and the only ultimate answers to the mystery of evil, bursting asunder the bonds of death, decline, and cultural aberration. But because grace works concretely in human subjectivity, the love of God poured into hearts by the Holy Spirit ultimately allows for the cultural community needed to reverse decline. Faith recognizes that God calls humans to the authenticity which overcomes evil with good, and so "faith is linked with human progress and it has to meet the challenge of human decline. For faith and progress have a common root in man's . . . self-transcendence. To promote either is to promote the other indirectly."[14] The predicament of our times is the predicament of cosmopolis, which requires a "new and higher collaboration of intellects through faith in God, that is, with a religiously and theologically transformed cosmopolis."[15]

11. Lonergan, *Collection*, 111.
12. Ibid.
13. Ibid., 111–12.
14. Lonergan, *Method*, 117.
15. Doran, *Theological Foundations*, 370.

Principle Four: An Education for Integration

Introducing faith might normally call for a conversation on the integration of faith and reason, but we do not approach the question in that manner, calling instead for a new model of integration, one integrating development from below upwards and development from above downwards.

The normal problem of integrating faith and reason often falls victim to the problems of faculty psychology, with various conceptual parts moved around like puzzle pieces until attaining some definitional fit. Take for example the problem of the noetic effects of sin, often treated as an abstraction that must be accounted for, but because abstract no more than a category, certainly not a concrete reality. An anthropology of the thinking thing is abstract, with conceptual and logical definitions, with the various "parts" of the human reality made overly distinct and thus in need of integration back into the concrete unity which is the human person. For Lonergan, however, there are always only complete human persons in their concrete subjectivity, and while subjectivity is historical, temporal, developmental, dynamic, and operates in various modes and differentiations, still there are only concrete subjects, and integration is a matter of authentic existence and coherence of actions, values, beliefs— an existential integration.

There is only the concrete subject, and as the subject develops he or she moves from inauthenticity to authenticity, but the single subject can develop in two distinct ways, from below upwards (achievement) and from above downwards (heritage).[16] Achievement is the development of consciousness from experience, to understanding, to correct judgment of facts, to value, and the source of development is immanent, the very dynamic desire and natural exigencies operative in the subject. Achievement "is the way of progress under the dynamism of human consciousness, of the drive to understand, to learn the truth, to respond to the deep, interior exigencies of our intelligent and rational and responsible nature."[17]

In history, such progress will become a "record of achievement," with the record made manifest in the various goods, institutions, systems, cultural symbolisms, artifacts, aesthetic products, moral codes,

16. Crowe, *Old Things and New*, 1–3.
17. Ibid., 1.

and religious accounts of human accomplishment. Subsequently, those achievements become "the inheritance of the human race . . . the accumulated patrimony of the community" handed on to others through the various forms of education, socialization, and enculturation operative in human community.[18] This is development from above downwards.

Development from above, heritage, begins with trust and belief—the child trusts the parent, the teacher, the school, the moral code, the religious authority—and so inherits the past achievements of others, which of course allows for cumulative progress in history since every person need not start new and discover everything from scratch. It is interesting to note, however, that the way of heritage begins not with data of experience, but with value, moving down to judgment, understanding, and then experience. Consider a loving family: the family exists as a community of love, parents for each other and for their children, and that love allows a child to trust their parents enough to believe what they say about having good manners, being obedient and respectful, following the rules and making their bed, as well as trusting the parents' statements about counting, the alphabet, what words signify, and so on. These beliefs are judgments, although probably not understood ones, about what is to be done and what is the case. In other words, the value of love allows the child to trust, and believe, judgments of value and fact. "Is this the case?" the child asks, and are told the answer, which they accept. A thoughtful child will eventually ask "Why?"—and the more thoughtful children will not stop asking—and will move from accepted judgments to an understanding of those judgments, understandings which they will be able to confirm for themselves in the data of experience. The process of development is thus an inverted image of achievement, for while the very same levels of experience, understanding, judging, and choosing are operating, the order is reversed.[19]

The pattern applies as well to faith, which for Lonergan is knowledge born of religious love.[20] Certainly the content of dogma is passed on as heritage, but faith in the sense meant here is a gift of God's love which floods hearts through the gift of God's Spirit.[21] This being-in-love is "knowledge reached through the discernment of value," an intentional

18. Ibid.
19. Ibid., 12–22.
20. Lonergan, *Method*, 115.
21. Ibid.

response to value, in this case a value revealed and bestowed by God.[22] As explained previously, the love of God shatters horizons, transvalues values, changes judgments, alters understanding, and expands experience. God's love precedes our knowledge of God, but the value given and apprehended is affirmed—"Yes!"—in judgments, which faith seeks to understand, and which leads to new lives and experience. Again, the up-and-down process continues, and these new lives and experiences can be questioned, understood, judged, and chosen as subsequent achievements.

This is all concrete, and it is all knowable through self-appropriation—we can discover our own development by adverting to our own subjectivity in self-appropriation, and this is hardly a rare or recondite reality but common and affirmed by the religiously converted. They also affirm that this development remakes their existence, allows self-transcendence and becomes the condition of their authenticity, and all in the very concrete ways that they live, move, and have their being in the world. This is all factical.

God's grace, on this model, operates in keeping with human nature—grace presupposes and perfects nature—rather than merely occupying a place in a flow chart of conceptual theology, but note that "a single structure of human consciousness guides each process, the way of progress moving from experience through understanding and judgment," and development from above "moving in the reverse direction. . . . It is this single structure, and the possibility of traversing it in either direction, that provides a real basis for the complementarity of the two ways."[23]

Consequently, the question of integration is "found in human nature itself, in the constants of the structure of consciousness, and in the variables of its development."[24] This shifts the conversation from the integration of faith and reason to the integration of two vectors of how a single structure develops, but there is no real contradiction or tension since development follows the same structures in the same concrete subjects. Further, in both vectors of development, the norms are identical—attentiveness, intelligence, reasonableness, responsibility, all

22. Ibid.
23. Crowe, *Old Things and New*, 2.
24. Ibid., 23.

in keeping with love, and all for the purpose of sustaining progress and reversing decline.

Education, whether secular or religious, has the same goals: the communication of intellectual development, the formation of a cultural community of cosmopolis, and the resultant human good in its various forms (vital, social, cultural, personal, religious), even if the reign of sin makes progress problematic and decline more than likely. But the integration of Christian education is the integration of self-transcending subjects, for God creates a "friendly universe" in which achievement and progress are not only possible, but also significant, for "man's good also is God's glory."[25] The purpose of the Christian university is to enable, as it can and in its own way, the collaboration of humans with each other and cooperation with God towards the goal of self-transcending love—authentic cosmopolitanism.

25. Lonergan, *Method*, 117.

Bibliography

Adler, Mortimer. *How to Think About the Great Ideas: From the Great Books of Western Civilization.* Chicago: Open Court, 2000.

Alexander, Larry, and Michael Moore. "Deontological Ethics." In *The Stanford Encyclopedia of Philosophy (Fall 2008 Edition),* edited by Edward N. Zalta. No pages. Online: http://plato.stanford.edu/archives/fall2008/entries/ethics-deontological/.

Anscombe, G. E. M. "Modern Moral Philosophy." *Philosophy* 33 (1958) 1–19.

Appiah, Kwame Anthony. *Cosmopolitanism: Ethics in a World of Strangers.* New York: W. W. Norton, 2006.

Aristotle. *The Nicomachean Ethics.* Translated by T. Irwin. Indianapolis: Hackett, 1999.

Arkes, Hadley. *First Things: An Inquiry into the First Principles of Morals and Justice.* Princeton: Princeton University Press, 1986.

Augustine. *The Confessions of Saint Augustine.* Translated by Rex Warner. New York: Signet Classic, 1963.

———. *Confessions.* Translated by Henry Chadwick. New York: Oxford University Press, 1991.

———. "Homily 7 on the First Epistle of John." In *Nicene and Post-Nicene Fathers,* translated by H. Browne, edited by Philip Schaff, First Series, Vol. 7. Buffalo, NY: Christian Literature, 1888. Revised and edited for New Advent by Kevin Knight. No pages. Online: http://www.newadvent.org/fathers/170207.htm.

———. *On Free Choice of the Will.* Translated by T. Williams. Indianapolis: Hackett Publishing, 1993.

———. *The Trinity.* Translated by Edmund Hill. New York: New City, 1991.

Baker, Deane-Peter. *Tayloring Reformed Epistemology: Charles Taylor, Alvin Plantinga and the de jure Challenge to Christian Belief.* London: SCM, 2007.

Bartholemew, Craig G., and Michael G. Goheen. *Living at the Crossroads: An Introduction to Christian Worldview.* Grand Rapids: Baker Academic, 2008.

Beaty, Michael D., and Douglas V. Henry. *The Schooled Heart: Moral Formation in American Higher Education.* Waco, TX: Baylor University Press, 2007.

Benhabib, Seyla. *Another Cosmopolitanism.* New York: Oxford University Press, 2006.

———. "Cosmopolitanism and Democracy: Affinities and Tensions." *The Hedgehog Review* 11 (2009) 30–41.

Benne, Robert. *Quality with Soul: How Six Premier Colleges and Universities Kept Faith with Their Religious Traditions.* Grand Rapids: Eerdmans, 2001.

The Big Lebowski. Directed by J. Coen. Produced by Polygram Filmed Entertainment. 1998.

Braman, Brian J. *Meaning and Authenticity: Bernard Lonergan and Charles Taylor on the Drama of Authentic Human Existence.* Toronto: University of Toronto Press, 2008.

Bringuier, Jean-Claude. *Conversations with Jean Piaget.* Translated by Basia Miller Gulati. Chicago: University of Chicago Press, 1969.

Brock, Stephen. "On Whether Aquinas' 'Ipsum Esse' is 'Platonism.'" *The Review of Metaphysics* 60 (2006) 269–303.

Burrell, David. "Analogy, Creation, and Theological Language." In *The Theology of Thomas Aquinas*, edited by R. van Nieuwenhove and J. Wawrykow, 77–98. Notre Dame: University of Notre Dame Press, 2005.

Burthaell, James Turnstead. *The Dying of the Light: The Disengagement of Colleges and Universities from their Christian Churches*. Grand Rapids: Eerdmans, 1998.

Byrne, Patrick H. "The Fabric of Lonergan's Thought." *Lonergan Workshop* 6 (1986) 1–84.

Cary, Phillip. *Augustine's Invention of the Inner Self: The Legacy of a Christian Platonist*. New York: Oxford University Press, 2000.

———. *Inner Grace: Augustine in the Tradition of Plato and Paul*. New York: Oxford University Press, 2008.

———. *Outward Signs: The Powerlessness of External Things in Augustine's Theology*. New York: Oxford University Press, 2008.

Cessario, Romanus. *A Short History of Thomism*. Washington, DC: Catholic University Press, 2003.

Clark, Gregory A. "The Nature of Conversion: How the Rhetoric of Worldview Philosophy Can Betray Evangelicals." In *The Nature of Confession: Evangelicals and Postliberals in Conversation*, by Timothy R. Phillips and Dennis L. Okholm, 201–18. Downers Grove: InterVarsity, 1996.

Cole, Robert W., and Paul D. Blankenstein. *Spirituality in Educational Leadership*. Thousand Oaks: Corwin, 2007.

Crowe, Frederick E. *Old Things and New: A Strategy for Education*. Atlanta: Scholars, 1985.

Cunningham, Conor. "Natura Pura, The Invention of the Anti-Christ: A Week with No Sabbath." *Communio* 37 (2010) 243–54.

Cunningham, David S. *To Teach, To Delight, and To Move: Theological Education in a Post-Christian World*. Eugene: Cascade, 2004.

Delanty, Gerard. *The Cosmopolitan Imagination: Critical Cosmopolitanism and Social Theory*. New York: Cambridge University Press, 2009.

Dickens, Charles. *A Tale of Two Cities*. New York: Penguin Classics, 2003.

Dill, Jeffrey S. "Cosmopolitanism: A Bibliographic Essay." *The Hedgehog Review* 11 (2009) 125–33.

Dockery, David S, and Gregory Alan Thornbury. *Shaping a Christian Worldview: The Foundations of Christian Higher Education*. Nashville: Broadman & Holman, 2002.

Dooyeweerd, Herman. *In the Twilight of Western Thought*. Nutley: Craig, 1980.

Doran, Robert M. *Theological Foundations*. 2 vols. Milwaukee: Marquette University Press, 1995.

Drilling, Peter. "The Psychological Analogy of the Trinity: Augustine, Aquinas, and Lonergan." *Irish Theological Quarterly* 71 (2006) 320–37.

Driver, Julia. *Ethics: The Fundamentals*. Malden, MA: Blackwell, 2007.

Dunaway, John Marson. *Gladly Teach, Gladly Learn: Living Out One's Calling in the Twenty-First Century Academy*. Macon: Macon University Press, 2005.

Evans, C. Stephen, and David Lyle Jeffrey. *The Bible and the University*. Grand Rapids: Zondervan, 2007.

Federici, Michael P. *Eric Voegelin*. Wilmington: ISI, 2002.

Flanagan, Joseph. *Quest for Self-Knowledge: An Essay in Lonergan's Philosophy*. Toronto: University of Toronto Press, 1997.

Freud, Sigmund. *Interpretation of Dreams: The Complete and Definitive Text.* Translated by J. Strachey. New York: Basic, 2010.

Frings, Manfred. *Max Scheler: A Concise Introduction into the World of a Great Thinker.* Pittsburgh: Duquesne University Press, 1965.

Goris, Harm. "Divine Foreknowledge, Providence, Predestination, and Human Freedom." In *The Theology of Thomas Aquinas,* edited by R. van Nieuwenhove and J. Wawrykow, 99–122. Notre Dame: University of Notre Dame Press, 2005.

Grecco, Richard. "Recent Ecclesiastical Teaching." In *John Paul II and Moral Theology,* edited by C. Curran and R. McCormick, 137–48. Mahwah, NJ: Paulist, 1998.

Griffiths, Paul. *Intellectual Appetite: A Theological Grammar.* Washington, DC: Catholic University of America Press, 2009.

Guignon, Charles. "Heidegger's 'Authenticity' Revisited." *Review of Metaphysics* 38 (1984) 331.

Gunton, Colin. "Augustine, The Trinity and the Theological Crisis of the West." *Scottish Journal of Theology* 43 (1990) 33–58.

Hadot, Pierre. *Philosophy as a Way of Life.* Translated by Michael Chase. Edited by Arnold I. Davidson. Malden, MA: Blackwell, 2005.

———. *What is Ancient Philosophy?* Translated by Michael Chase. Cambridge, MA: Belknap, 2002.

Hamilton, Michael S., and James A. Mathisen. "Faith and Learning at Wheaton College." In *Models for Christian Higher Education: Strategies for Success in the Twenty-First Century,* edited by Richard T. Hughes and William B. Adrian, 261–83. Grand Rapids: Eerdmans, 1997.

Hanby, Michael. *Augustine and Modernity.* New York: Routledge, 2003.

Hauerwas, Stanley. *The State of the University: Academic Knowledges and Knowledge of God.* Malden: Blackwell, 2007.

Hays, Richard B. *The Moral Vision of the New Testament: A Contemporary Introduction to New Testament Ethics.* New York: HarperOne, 1996.

Heidegger, Martin. "Augustine and Neo-Platonism." In *The Phenomenology of Religious Life,* translated by Matthias Fritsch and Jennifer Anna Gosetti-Ferencei, 115–84. Bloomington: Indiana University Press, 2004.

———. *Being and Time.* Translated by J. Macquarrie and E. Robinson. San Francisco: HarperSanFrancisco, 1962.

Hildebrand, Dietrich von. *Christian Ethics.* New York: David McKay, 1953.

Hoitenga, Dewey J., Jr. "The Noetic Effects of Sin: A Review Article." *Calvin Theological Journal* 38 (2003) 68–102.

Holmes, Arthur F. *Building the Christian Academy.* Grand Rapids: Eerdmans, 2001.

———. *The Idea of a Christian College.* Grand Rapids: Eerdmans, 1975.

Houston, Paul D., Alan M. Blankstein, and Robert W. Cole. *Spirituality in Educational Leadership.* Thousand Oaks: Corwin Press, 2008.

Hughes, Richard T., and William B. Adrian. *Models for Christian Higher Education: Strategies for Success in the Twenty-First Century.* Grand Rapids: Eerdmans, 1997.

Hughes, Richard T. *The Vocation of a Christian Scholar.* Rev. ed. Grand Rapids: Eerdmans, 2005.

Hunt, Anne. *What Are They Saying About the Trinity.* New York: Paulist, 1998.

Hursthouse, Rosalind. "Virtue Ethics." In *The Stanford Encyclopedia of Philosophy (Winter 2010 Edition),* edited by Edward N. Zalta, no pages. Online: http://plato .stanford.edu/archives/win2010/entries/ethics-virtue/.

Jacobsen, Douglas, and Rhonda Hustedt Jacobsen. *The American University in a Postsecular Age*. Oxford: Oxford University Press, 2008.

Jacobsen, Rhonda Hustedt, and Douglas Jacobsen. *Scholarship and Christian Faith: Enlarging the Conversation*. New York: Oxford University Press, 2004.

John Paul II. *Man and Woman He Created Them: A Theology Of The Body*. Translated by Michael Waldstein. Boston: Pauline Books and Media, 2006.

Kanaris, Jim, and Mark J. Doorley. *In Deference to the Other: Lonergan and Contemporary Continental Thought*. Albany: State University of New York Press, 2004.

Kant, Immanuel. *Critique of Pure Reason*. Edited by P. Guyer and A. Wood. Cambridge: Cambridge University Press, 1989.

———. *Religion within the Limits of Reason Alone*. Translated by T. Greene and H. Hudson. San Francisco: Harper Torchbooks, 1960.

Kerr, Fergus. *After Aquinas: Versions of Thomism*. Malden, MA: Wiley-Blackwell, 2002.

Keys, Mary M. *Aquinas, Aristotle, and the Promise of the Common Good*. New York: Cambridge University Press, 2006.

Kilby, Karen. "Aquinas, the Trinity and the Limits of Understanding." *International Journal of Systematic Theology* 7 (2005) 414–27.

Lawrence, Frederick G. "Expanding Challenge to Authenticity in *Insight*: Lonergan's Hermeneutics of Facticity (1953–1964)." *Divyadaan* 15 (2004) 427–56.

———. "The Fragility of Consciousness: Lonergan and the Postmodern Concern for the Other." *Theological Studies* 54 (1993) 55–94.

———. "The Hermeneutic Revolution and the Future of Theology." In *Between the Human and the Divine: Philosophical and Theological Hermeneutics*, edited by Andrzei Wiercinski, 326–54. Toronto: Hermeneutic, 2002.

———. "Lonergan and Aquinas: The Postmodern Problematic of Theology and Ethics." In *The Ethics of Aquinas*, edited by Stephen J. Pope, 437–55. Washington, DC: Georgetown University Press, 2002.

———. "Lonergan, the Integral Postmodern." *Method: Journal of Lonergan Studies* 18 (2000) 95–122.

Litfin, Duane. *Conceiving the Christian College*. Grand Rapids: Eerdmans, 2004.

Lonergan, Bernard. *Collection*. Edited by F. Crowe. Toronto: University of Toronto Press, 1988.

———. *Grace and Freedom: Operative Grace in the Thought of St. Thomas Aquinas*. Edited by R. Doran and F. Crowe. Vol. 1, *Collected Works of Bernard Lonergan*. Toronto: University of Toronto Press, 2000.

———. *Insight: A Study of Human Understanding*. Edited by Frederick Crowe and Robert Doran. Vol. 3, *Collected Works of Bernard Lonergan*. Toronto: University of Toronto Press, 1992.

———. *Method in Theology*. Toronto: University of Toronto Press, 1971.

———. "Natural Right and Historical Mindedness." In *Third Collection: Papers by Bernard J. F. Lonergan, S.J.*, edited by F. Crowe, 169–83. New York: Paulist, 1985.

———. *Philosophical and Theological Papers, 1965-1980*. Edited by R. Croken and R. Doran. Vol. 17, *Collected Works of Bernard Lonergan*. Toronto: University of Toronto Press, 2004.

———. "Regis College Institute 'On the Method of Theology' 9–20 July 1962." In *Early Works on Theological Method* 1, edited by R. Doran and R. Croken, 128–54. Vol. 22, *Collected Works of Bernard Lonergan*. Toronto: University of Toronto Press, 2010.

———. "The Role of a Catholic University in the Modern World." In *Collection*, edited by F. Crowe and R. Doran, 108–13. Vol. 4, *Collected Works of Bernard Lonergan*. Toronto: Toronto University Press, 1988.

———. *A Second Collection*. Edited by W. Ryan and B. Tyrrell. Toronto: University of Toronto Press, 1974.

———. "Self-Transcendence: Intellectual, Moral, Religious." In *Philosophical and Theological Papers, 1965-1980*, edited by R. Croken and R. Doran, 313–31. Vol. 17, *Collected Works of Bernard Lonergan*. Toronto: University of Toronto Press, 2004.

———. "The Subject." In *The Lonergan Reader*, edited by Mark D. Morelli and Elizabeth A. Morelli, 420–35. Toronto: University of Toronto Press, 1997.

———. "The Subject." In *A Second Collection: Papers by Bernard J. F. Lonergan, S.J.* Edited by W. Ryan and B. Tyrrell, 69–86. Toronto: University of Toronto Press, 1974.

———. *Topics in Education*. Edited by R. Doran and F. Crowe. Toronto: University of Toronto Press, 1993.

———. *The Triune God: Systematics*. Edited by R. Doran et. al. Toronto: University of Toronto Press, 2009.

———. *Understanding and Being: The Halifax Lectures on "Insight"*. Edited by E. Morelli and M. Morelli. Toronto: University of Toronto, 1990.

———. "Unity and Plurality." In *Third Collection: Papers by Bernard J. F. Lonergan, S. J.*, edited by F. Crowe, 239–50. New York: Paulist Press, 1985.

———. *Verbum: Word and Idea in Aquinas*. Edited by Frederick E. Crowe and Robert M. Doran. Vol. 2, *Collected Works of Bernard Lonergan*. Toronto: University of Toronto Press, 1997.

Long, Stephen. *Natura Pura: On the Recovery of Nature in the Doctrine of Grace*. 2nd ed. New York: Fordham University Press, 2010.

Loyola, Ignatius. *"Spiritual Exercises" and Selected Works*. Translated and edited by G. Ganss. New York: Paulist, 1991.

Lubac, Henri de. *Surnaturel: Études historiques*. Edited by M. Sales. Paris: Desclée de Brouwer, 1991.

MacIntyre, Alasdair. *God, Philosophy, Universities*. Notre Dame: University of Notre Dame, 2009.

Manent, Pierre. *The City of Man*. Translated by Marc A. LePain. Princeton: Princeton University Press, 1998.

———. *An Intellectual History of Liberalism*. Translated by Rebecca Balinksi. Princeton: Princeton University Press, 1995.

Marsh, James L. "Self-Appropriation and Liberation." *Proceedings of the American Catholic Philosophical Association* 79 (2005) 1–18.

Maslow, Abraham. *Motivation and Personality*. New York: Harper, 1954.

———. *Religions, Values and Peak Experiences*. New York: Viking, 1970.

———. *Toward a Psychology of Being*. 2nd ed. New York: Van Nostrand Reinhold, 1968.

Matustik, Martin. "Democratic Multicultures and Cosmopolis: Beyond the Aporias of the Politics of Identity and Difference." *Method: Journal of Lonergan Studies* 12 (1994) 63–89.

McCool, Gerald A. *The Neo-Thomists*. Milwaukee: Marquette University Press, 1994.

McPartland, Thomas J. *Lonergan and the Philosophy of Historical Existence*. Columbia: University of Missouri Press, 2001.

Melleby, Donald Ortiz and Derek. *The Outrageous Idea of Academic Faithfulness.* Grand Rapids: Brazos, 2007.

Middleton, J. Richard, and Brian J. Walsh. *The Transforming Vision: Shaping a Christian Worldview.* Downers Grove, IL: IVP, 1984.

Milbank, John. *Theology and Social Theory: Beyond Secular Reason.* 2nd ed. Malden, MA: Wiley-Blackwell, 2006.

Milosz, Czselaw. *The Captive Mind.* New York: Vintage, 1990.

Monan, J. Donald. "Value Proposition." In *Boston College Magazine* (Summer 2009). No pages. Online: http://bcm.bc.edu/issues/summer_2009/features/value-proposition.html.

Moroney, Stephen K. "How Sin Affects Scholarship: A New Model." *Christian Scholars Review* 28 (1995) 432–51.

———. *The Noetic Effects of Sin: A Historical and Contemporary Exploration of How Sin Affects our Thinking.* Lanham: Lexington, 2000.

Naugle, David K. *Worldview: The History of a Concept.* Grand Rapids: Eerdmans, 2002.

Nettleship, Richard Lewis. *The Theory of Education in Plato's Republic.* Oxford: Clarendon Press, 1935.

Niebuhr, Reinhold. *The Nature and Destiny of Man.* New York: Scribner's, 1941.

Nordquest, David A. "Cosmopolis: Bourget's and Lonergan's." *Method: Journal of Lonergan Studies* 11 (1993) 37–50.

Ormerod, Neil. "Augustine and the Trinity: Whose Crisis?" *Pacifica* 16 (2003) 17–32.

———. "The Psychological Analogy for the Trinity: At Odds with Modernity." *Pacifica* 14 (2001) 281–94.

———. *The Trinity: Retrieving the Western Tradition.* Milwaukee: Marquette University Press, 2005.

Pally, Marcia. *The New Evangelicals: Expanding the Vision of the Common Good.* Grand Rapids: Eerdmans, 2011.

Pearcey, Nancy. *Total Truth: Liberating Christianity from Its Cultural Captivity.* Wheaton, IL: Crossway, 2005.

Piaget, Jean. *The Essential Piaget.* Edited by H. Gruber and J. Vonèche. New York: Basic, 1977.

Pieper, Josef. *A Brief Reader on the Virtues of the Human Heart.* Translated by P. Duggan. San Francisco: Ignatius, 1991.

Plantinga, Alvin. *Warranted Christian Belief.* New York: Oxford University Press, 2000.

Plantinga, Cornelius, Jr. *Engaging God's World: A Christian Vision of Faith, Learning, and Living.* Grand Rapids: Eerdmans, 2002.

Plants, Nicolas. "Decentering Inwardness." In *In Deference to the Other: Lonergan and Contemporary Continental Thought,* edited by J. Kanaris and M. Doorley, 13–32. Albany: State University of New York Press, 2004.

———. "Lonergan and Taylor: A Critical Integration." *Method: Journal of Lonergan Studies* 19 (2001) 143–72.

Plato. "Phaedo ." In *The Collected Dialogues of Plato.* Edited by Edith Hamilton and Huntington Cairns. Princeton: Princeton University Press, 1961.

———. *The Republic of Plato.* Translated by Allan Bloom. New York: Basic, 1968.

Polt, Richard. *Heidegger: An Introduction.* Ithaca: Cornell University Press, 1999.

Rommen, Heinrich. *The Natural Law: A Study in Legal and Social History and Philosophy.* Indianapolis: Liberty Fund, 1998.

Schaeffer, Francis. *Escape from Reason.* Downers Grove, IL: IVP, 1968.

―――. *How Should We Then Live: The Rise and Decline of Western Thought and Culture.* Wheaton, IL: Crossway, 1976.

Schwehn, Mark R. *Exiles from Eden: Religion and the Academic Vocation in America.* New York: Oxford University Press, 1993.

Seerveld, Calvin. *A Christian Critique of Art and Literature.* Toronto: Tuppence, 1995.

Simpson, Christopher. *Religion, Metaphysics, and the Postmodern: William Desmond and John D. Caputo.* Bloomington: Indiana University Press, 2009.

Sinnott-Armstrong, Walter. "Consequentialism." In *The Stanford Encyclopedia of Philosophy (Winter 2011 Edition)*, edited by Edward N. Zalta, no pages. Online: http://plato.stanford.edu/archives/win2011/entries/consequentialism/.

Sire, James W. *Naming the Elephant: Worldview as a Concept.* Downers Grove, IL: Inter Varsity, 2004.

―――. *The Universe Next Door: A Basic Worldview Catalogue.* 5th ed. Downers Grove: Intervarsity, 2004.

Smith, Christian. *Moral, Believing Animals: Human Personhood and Culture.* New York: Oxford University Press, 2003.

Smith, James K. A. *Desiring the Kingdom: Worship, Worldview, and Cultural Formation.* Grand Rapids: Baker Academic, 2009.

―――. *Introducing Radical Orthodoxy: Mappiing a Post-Secular Theology.* Grand Rapids: Baker Academic, 2004.

Smith, Nicholas H. *Charles Taylor: Meaning, Morals and Modernity.* Malden: Polity, 2002.

Snell, R. J. "Making Men without Chests: The Intellectual Life and Moral Imagination." *First Principles* (February 25, 2010). No pages. Online: http://www.firstprinciplesjournal.com/articles.aspx?article=1380.

―――. "Thomism and Noetic Sin, Transposed: A Response to Neo-Calvinist Objections." *Philosophia Christi* 12 (2010) 7–28.

―――. *Through a Glass Darkly: Bernard Lonergan and Richard Rorty on Knowing without a God's-eye View.* Milwaukee: Marquette University Press, 2006.

Snell, R. J., and Kurt W. Peterson. "'Faith Forms the Intellectual Task': The Pietist Option in Christian Higher Education." In *The Pietist Impulse in Christianity*, edited by Christian T. Collins Winn et al., 215–30. Eugene: Pickwick, 2011.

Solberg, Richard W. *Lutheran Higher Education in North America.* Minneapolis: Augsburg, 1985.

Sommerville, C. John. *The Decline of the Secular University.* Oxford: Oxford University Press, 2006.

Spears, Paul D., and Steven R. Loomis. *Education for Human Flourishing: A Christian Perspective.* Downers Grove, IL: Intervarsity, 2009.

Stebbins, J. Michael. *The Divine Initiative: Grace, World Order, and Human Freedom in the Early Writings of Bernard Lonergan.* Toronto: University of Toronto Press, 1995.

Szelényi, Katalin, and Robert A. Rhoads. *Global Citizenship and the University: Advancing Social Life and Relations in an Interdependent World.* Stanford: Stanford University Press, 2011.

Taylor, Charles. "Engaged Agency and Background in Heidegger." In *The Cambridge Companion to Heidegger*, edited by Charles Guignon, 317–36. Cambridge: Cambridge University Press, 1993.

―――. *The Ethics of Authenticity.* Cambridge: Harvard University Press, 1991.

―――. *Multiculturalism: Examining the Politics of Recognition.* Princeton: Princeton University Press, 1994.

———. *Philosophical Arguments.* Cambridge: Harvard University Press, 1995.

———. *A Secular Age.* Cambridge: Belknap Press, 2007.

———. *Sources of the Self: The Making of the Modern Identity.* Cambridge: Harvard University Press, 1989.

Thiselton, Anthony. *The Two Horizons: New Testament Hermeneutics and Philosophical Description.* Grand Rapids: Eerdmans, 1980.

Thomas Aquinas. *Summa Theologica.* 5 vols. Translated by Fathers of the English Dominican Province. Allen, TX: Christian Classics, 1981.

Tracy, David. *The Achievement of Bernard Lonergan.* New York: Herder and Herder, 1970.

Turner, James, and Mark A. Noll. *The Future of Christian Learning: An Evangelical and Catholic Dialogue.* Grand Rapids: Brazos, 2008.

Voegelin, Eric. *Anamnesis.* Translated by Gerhart Niemeyer. Columbia: University of Missouri Press, 1978.

———. *The Beginning and the Beyond: A Meditation on Truth.* Vol. 28, *The Collected Works of Eric Voegelin,* edited by Thomas A. Hollweck and Paul Caringella. Baton Rouge: Louisiana State University Press, 1990.

———. *The History of the Race Idea.* Translated by Ruth Hein. Columbia: University of Missouri Press, 1998.

———. *Plato.* Baton Rouge: Louisiana State University Press, 1966.

Vos, Arvin. *Aquinas, Calvin, and Contemporary Protestant Thought: A Critique of Protestant Views on the Thought of Thomas Aquinas.* Washington, DC: Christian College Consortium, 1985.

Wells, Ronald A., and Janel M. Curry. *Faithful Imagination in the Academy: Eplorations in Religious Belief and Scholarship.* Lanham: Lexington, 2008.

West, Christopher. *Theology of the Body Explained.* Boston: Pauline Books and Media, 2003.

Westphal, Merold. *Overcoming Onto-theology: Toward a Postmodern Christian Faith.* New York: Fordham University Press, 2001.

Wilson, Woodrow. "Princeton in the Nation's Service: A Commemorative Address Delivered on October 21, 1896." No pages. Online: http://www.princeton.edu/~mudd/exhibits/wilsonline/indn8nsvc.html

Wolters, Albert M. *Creation Regained: Biblical Basics for a Reformational Worldview.* 2nd Edition. Grand Rapids: Eerdmans, 2005.

Wolterstorff, Nicholas. *Educating for Shalom: Essays on Christian Higher Education.* Edited by Clarence W. Joldersma and Gloria Gloris Stronks. Grand Rapids: Eerdmans, 2004.

———. *Justice: Rights and Wrongs.* Princeton: Princeton University Press, 2008.

Wright, John, and Michael Budde. *Conflicting Allegiances: The Church-Based University in a Liberal Democratic Society.* Grand Rapids: Brazos, 2004.

Yates, Joshua J. "Mapping the Good World: The New Cosmopolitans and our Changing Word Picture." *The Hedgehog Review* 11 (2009) 7–27.